INDIA'S FOREIGN TRADE

INDIA'S FOREIGN TRADE
From Antiquity to Date

Mahesh Prasad

KALPAZ

India's Foreign Trade from Antiquity to Date

ISBN: 978-81-7835-907-6

Published in 2011 in India by
Kalpaz Publications
C-30, Satyawati Nagar,
Delhi-110052
E-mail: kalpaz@hotmail.com
Phone : 9212729499

Lasser Type Setting : Quick Media, Delhi
Printed at : Chawla Offset Printers, Delhi

Contents

Preface

India is fast emerging as a major force in the world economy, next only to China. Many scholars have pointed out that over the next two decades, India and China will emerge as super powers.

Back in the early Fifties, India was a young State, still in the process of building its economy. In those days, India's position in the world trade was insignificant. As would be apparent, the idea behind the book has been to study the export potential of each commodity, as also the countries which attract heavy import from India, both quantity-wise and value-wise.

The study deals with different items of import and export, which will be of great interest to those involved in industrial and agricultural production in the country. Items that are in great demand require large-scale production. Further, these very items may have equally large demand within the country. This will require greater attention, as only surplus can be exported.

While India's foreign trade in the ancient, medieval and modern periods have been dealt with by different authors, trade during the contemporary period—from 1960-61 onwards—has barely been dealt with, expect by one author. The present work has been an attempt to bridge this gap.

As would be apparent, writing a treatise of this nature involved a great deal of research. It involved collecting data from several government agencies and trade bodies.

The present work deals not only with commodities, but also with the service sector, as also barter, which began gaining momentum during the recent global economic slowdown.

I would like to acknowledge help from Dr. Baldeo Sahai, an author of about a dozen books, who lent me invaluable advice and to my daughter, Swati Prasad, for going through the manuscript.

Author

Introduction

India's trade with the outside world dates back to the earliest of times. No doubt, trade in volumes can be traced only to the medieval period and to the arrival of European Powers. Nonetheless, trade flourished in antiquity.

India, rated as one of the oldest civilizations of the world, witnessed flourishing trade with neighbouring countries and regions as far back as 7th century B.C. Diggings at the ancient Egyptian port town of Berenike have produced spices and gem fragments that prove that Indian goods routinely made their way to Egypt.

Ibn Batuta, the 14th century Moorish traveler and Duarte Barbosa, a Portuguese official in Cochin in early 14th century, found many cotton trade centers in India, which were famous for their textiles. Textile products from Gujarat were exported to Arabian countries and to South-east Asia. The products included quilts of embroidered tussar or munga, or cotton, or jute, or silk. Malabar in Kerala was famous for its coloured and printed cloth material.

Hardwood furniture, embellished with inlay work, was a very popular item. Carpet-weaving touched new heights in the Mughal era. The affinity of the Great Mughals with nature is evident from the designs of the carpets made during that period. It was, however, in the late 20th and 21st centuries that trade was pursued in great volumes and value. Data on commodity-wise and country-wise trade is available with the Directorate General of Commercial Intelligence and Statistics (DGCI & S), Ministry of Commerce, Government of India, from 1960-61 onwards.

The year 2005 marks a milestone in the merchandise exports of the country. It was in 2005 that India's exports reached one per cent of world exports from the level of 0.67 per cent in 2000-01 and remaining unchanged at 0.8 per cent between 2003 and 2004. India's share went up further to 1.1 per cent in 2007 and remained at that level in 2008. Further, it reached 1.2 per cent in 2009 (January-June), according to the Economic Survey 2009-10.

Although the country's merchandise exports registered a growth of 20 per cent plus in dollar terms since 2002-03, the global recession jolted the continued upward thrust with a growth rate of 3.6 per cent for 2008-09. Nevertheless, according to revised figures, export growth in 2008-09 stood at 13.6 per cent, which indicates that India withstood the crisis better than other countries.

The "Medium Term Export Strategy 2002-07", released in 2002 had stressed the urgent need to raise the share of India's exports to at least one per cent of the world exports "in the next five years." This has now been achieved sooner than targeted. Also, for the first time in 2005, "India's export growth surpassed that of China," which has been recognized as a stellar export performer for years.

This should not, however, make the powers that be complacent, as the country's rivals, particularly China has all along been doing better and would still make an effort to outdo India. Moreover, all along India's imports have exceeded its exports. China has, in recent years, relied with success on export-led growth. It has imported iron ore, plastic and rubber in large quantities as raw material from India for manufacture and exports of finished goods. Further, India's exports have been affected by a rising rupee in relation to the US dollar. The rupee's 15 per cent rise against the dollar has almost entirely eaten away the margin the exporters made from US shipments.

India's escalating imports are to quite a large extent due to India's need for oil, whose prices in the international market have been going up. Not to be taken in by the intensity of its need for oil, India is planning to become a major exporter of petroleum products and to use the export earnings to partly cover its import bill. An "Export-Blueprint," drawn up by the Petroleum Ministry envisages converting the present and the planned coastal refineries into export-oriented refineries with large capacities so that export earnings pay for import of crude oil.

Under the new strategy, coastal refineries, which are economic and competitive when compared to neighbouring overseas refineries, would be equipped to focus on exports, while new inland refineries would be built soon to meet the hinterland demand-supply gap. Currently, the government incurs huge expenditure on account of moving petroleum products from coastal refineries to hinterland.

Foreign trade, particularly exports, are important for the growth potential of any country. As has been pointed out earlier, several countries including China, have in recent years relied with success on export-led growth. India too is making efforts in this direction, but its imports continue to exceed its exports. Some imports, like machinery and equipment, are essential for the country's development as also exports, and have to be imported in any case. Still, India would do well to stress on value-added exports, rather than exports of raw materials, although this has to be done till we have increased capability to produce finished goods as domestic demand is mounting with higher purchasing power of the people.

In the initial years after independence, say during 1951-60, India's exports were sluggish, whereas imports had to be carried out to meet the nation's requirements, both for essential consumer goods and capital goods. Thus, while exports financed 83.4 per cent of imports during the First Five Year Plan, the proportion came down to 56 per cent during the Second Plan. The mounting requirements of imports have had to be financed by a large-scale withdrawal from India's foreign exchange reserves, accumulated during the Second World War and massive external assistance during the ten-year period, 1951-1960. The country's sterling balances were drawn down by Rs. 7,360 million; and in addition charge India utilized, up to 31st March 1961, external assistance (excluding drawings on the IMF) worth Rs. 16,944 million, writes Dr. Manmohan Singh in his book "India's Export Trends and Prospects for Self-sustained Growth."

The situation changed somewhat during the five-year period beginning 1972-73, when the export growth averaged 26.2 per cent. Imports during the period too registered high growth, particularly during 1973-74 and 1974-75, when they showed growth of 58.3 per cent and 52.9 per cent respectively. Nevertheless, the average import growth during the five year period was contained at 28.58 per cent. Although during the three years, beginning 2002-03, export growth has been over 20 per cent in US dollar terms, import growth too has been hefty, mainly because of the need for oil imports.

India's merchandise exports have expanded vastly over the last five decades. From the level of Rs. 6,420 million in 1960-61, India's exports have gone up to Rs. 8,407,550 million in 2008-09 from Rs. 8,640,655 million in the previous year and Rs. 4,564,178 million in 2005-06 — over 710 times. Imports too have grown much faster and have been much higher in value terms – from Rs.11,220 million in 1960-61 to Rs. 6,604,088.99 million in 2005-06. However, growth in exports of over 20 per cent during three years since 2002-03 have surpassed targets. In 2004-05, export growth was a high of 26.2 per cent, the highest since 1975-76 and the second highest since 1950-51. In dollar terms, exports crossed the US $80 billion mark in 2004-05. Export growth in 2005-06 was 23.4 per cent, which helped the country cross the US $100 billion mark. Merchandise imports grew by a much higher rate of 33.8 per cent to US $149.2 billion, leaving a net trade deficit of US $49.2 billion, emphasizing the need of further growth in exports. The trend of high growth rate in exports was continued in 2006-07. As stated earlier "The global recession jolted this continued upward growth with initial estimates showing a growth rate of 3.6 per cent for 2008-09," says Economic Survey 2009-10.

India's significant export growth in recent years was on account of a host of favourable external developments and domestic policy initiatives. Improved global growth and recovery in world trade aided the growth of India's exports. The opening up of the economy and corporate restructuring has enhanced the competitiveness of the Indian industry. There is the need, therefore, to study the export potential of each item as also of factors, which hinder export growth of the item and measures needed to propel exports.

India is also seeking to promote exports through regional groupings, like BIMSTEK (Bangladesh, India, Myanmar, Sri Lanka and Thailand, initially, and now including Bhutan and Nepal too), ASEAN+2 (ASEAN, New Zealand and Australia) and IBSA (India, Brazil and South Africa). On a visit to South Africa in the middle of October, 2007, to review the progress of the state of play of the Doha round, India's Prime Minister, Dr. Manmohan Singh, sought to forge the closest possible cooperation with the two other IBSA countries. Dr Singh said, "India, Brazil and South Africa should achieve a trade target of US $30 billion by 2012."

Dr. Singh said, "We have set ourselves a modest target of US $15 billion by 2010 for trade among our three countries. My suggestion to our business leaders would be to aim to achieve this by 2009 and then to go on to double that by 2012, Business must be proactive," he told the second IBSA summit, held in Pretoria.

Recently, with the normalization of relations, Pakistan too is keen to import from India commodities, which it was buying from distant countries at much higher prices. It is significant that besides essential commodities, like tea, Pakistan happened to be one of the major markets for rubber products, fruits and vegetable seeds, soft drinks other than lemonade. It also imported from India during 2004-05 and 2005-06, among others, sugar crisp bread, corn flakes and malt extracts. India needs to cultivate, not only Pakistan, but other neighbouring, Asian and African countries too, to buy more from India.

Exports can broadly be classified into 'Agriculture and allied products', non-fuel primary items, like ores, minerals and metals, including 'ores and minerals (excluding coal)', 'manufactured goods' and mineral fuels and lubricants (including coal). Among agriculture and allied products, the traditional items like tea, coffee, tobacco and spices have not shown as much growth as manufactured goods. Ores and minerals (including coal) have on the other hand shown good growth. Among agricultural and allied products, export of wheat emerged as a new item in recent years. However, exports of the item depends upon crop prospects.

Agriculture and allied products exports can further be classified into perishable and non-perishable. Perishable items include fresh fruits and vegetable products, meat and meat preparations, marine products, dairy, poultry and floriculture products. Among non-perishables are an array of products, including tea, coffee, spices, tobacco, food grains, gur, molasses, cashew, groundnut, oil meals shellac, processed vegetables and processed fruits and juices.

There has been a stupendous growth in India's exports of agriculture and allied products in value terms since 1960-61, when they stood at a meager Rs. 2,840 million. Exports of these items have gone up to Rs. 467,030 million in 2005-06, registering a high growth rate. Exports of tea have gone up in value terms, although in volume terms there is a decline. India exported 199,200 tons of tea, valued at Rs. 1,240 million in 1960-61, but only 183,403 tons, valued at Rs. 18,402.98 million in 2004-05.

In the case of coffee, tobacco and spices, however, there is growth, both in value and quantitative terms. In food grains, India is a major exporter of Basmati rice, the flavoured one, which is a favourite. India's exports of wheat has shown an uptrend since 2000-01. Export of wheat, which was 632,468 tons, valued at Rs. 3,667.6 million in 1995-96, went up to 4,022,705 tons valued at Rs. 23,493.7 million in 2003-04, when it reached its peak. Exports of other cereals, which include rye, maize, bajra, jowar, ragi and sorghum, recorded an increase of 469.5 per cent in terms of quantity and 336.08 per cent in terms of value in 2003-04 over the previous year.

Agricultural exports of the country have, however, shown a declining trend in the last few years. Agricultural and allied products exports as a percentage of total exports, which were 11.9 per cent in 2003-04, declined to 10.5 per cent in 2004-05 and further to 10.2 per cent in 2005-06.

APEDA (Agricultural Products Export Development Authority) assists promotions of exports of floriculture, fresh fruits and vegetables, processed fruits and vegetables, buffalo meat, sheep/goat meat, poultry products, dairy products, processed meats, peanuts, cocoa products, cereal preparations, alcoholic and non-alcoholic beverages, and non-basmati rice. Over 50 per cent of market development efforts are in the Middle East, followed by Europe, Japan, the United States, Brazil, Indonesia and Malaysia.

Exports of ores and minerals (excluding coal) have gone up from Rs. 520 million in 1960-61 to Rs. 237,330 million in 2005-06. Exports of manufactured goods have shown a similar rise from Rs. 2,910 million in 1960-61 to Rs. 3,285,070 million in 2005-06. Exports of mineral fuels and lubricants (including coal) have gone up from Rs. 70 million to Rs. 525,380 million during the period.

In 2005-06, India's exports of manufactured goods grew by 19.6 per cent and had a share of around 72 per cent in total exports. Within manufacturing, the high performers were engineering goods (mainly manufactures of metals, machinery and instruments, transport equipment, primary and semi-finished iron and steel and non-ferrous metals); gems and jewelry; and chemicals and related products (including basic chemicals, pharmaceuticals and cosmetics), plastics, linoleum and rubber, glass and other products and residual chemicals and allied products). Of late, however, there has been a deceleration in the growth of gems and jewelry.

In textiles, despite the new opportunities that opened up with the phasing out of textiles quotas, textiles exports have shown a disappointing negative growth. Still, with quota regime giving way to free market at the global level at the beginning of 2005, there is a lot of expectation from the Indian textile industry. So far, while China's performance exceeded expectations, India's performance has not been satisfactory.

One notable feature of export growth was the growth in project goods by more than 200 per cent. From a modest beginning in the late 1970s, project exports have evolved over the years to reflect the country's technological maturity and industrial capabilities; give visibility to Indian technical expertise, project execution capability and create entry points for other firms for supplies, consultancy and manpower exports. Exports of projects and services, including construction and industrial turnkey projects and consultancy services increased from US $629 million in 1998-99 to US $911 million in 2004-05.

Further gains in exports require a deepening of domestic reforms, and an accelerated removal of infrastructure bottlenecks, including export infrastructure. Infrastructure remains the single most important constraint to export growth. Achievement of ambitious export target in India's Foreign Trade Policy (2004-09) requires a projected augmentation of the installed capacity of ports by 140 per cent. Indian ports, which handle over 70 per cent of India's foreign trade, have a turn-around time of 3-5 days as against 4-6 hours at international ports, like Singapore and Hong Kong. As for internal transport, while there has been a perceptible improvement in national highways, secondary roads need to be improved and the issue of delays caused at interstate check points need to be addressed.

"The book also deals with barter where goods are exchanged for goods without bringing in money. India has been carrying on barter trade among others with China and Mynmar since antiquity. The current global recession has

fuelled barter trade and the trend is gaining momentum in India too. In today's internet economy, barter is being promoted by B2B portals which is giving a new life to barter."

As trade grows and the number of consignments increases, there is need not only for improved trade infrastructure, but also for streamlining trade data to remove any data anomalies and provide the basis for appropriate policy formulation. Exporters need to place more emphasis on non-price factors like product quality, brand image, packaging, delivery and after-sales service. A more aggressive push to FDI in export industries will not only increase the rate of investment in the economy, but also infuse new technologies and management practices in these industries. Equally important is the availability of adequate export credit at competitive rates.

Direction of Trade

To expand the country's exports, it is essential to tap markets with good growth potential. In the case of India, the share of its 11 major trading partners, accounting for around 48 per cent in its trade, has not changed much since 2000-01. The USA continues to be the single largest trading partner of India. However, its share has fallen in 2004-05. China has emerged as the second major trading partner in 2005-06 and the share of China-Hong Kong at 9.4 per cent was close to that of the USA (10 per cent). UAE is the next major trading partner. Another important country, whose share has been increasing steadily, is Singapore, with which India has signed a Comprehensive Economic Cooperation Agreement (CECA).

Region-wise, India's exports to Asia and Oceania (with a share of 45.4 per cent) registered a robust growth of 27 per cent in 2004-05. This was powered by the high growth in exports to China, Singapore, UAE and Republic of Korea. The other two major regions – EU-25 and America (with share of 21.7 per cent and 20.4 per cent respectively) registered a growth of 20 per cent. Exports to Africa and Latin America were also impressive.

The growing importance of Asia in India's exports indicates that the regional trading arrangements (RTAs) strategy is bearing fruit. Framework Agreements on economic cooperation have also been entered into with MERCOSUR and Chile. India is also engaged with Gulf Cooperation Council and Mauritius for FTA/Comprehensive Economic Cooperation Partnership Agreement and India-Israel and India-Brazil, South Africa (IBSA) joint Study Groups have also been set up.

Foreign Trade Policy

To promote exports, and to take an integrated view of overall development of foreign trade the Indian Government has been announcing Foreign Trade Policy, the last one was for the period 2009-14, announced on August 27, 2009. The basic objective of this policy is to double India's share in world trade and to make exports an effective instrument of economic growth. The annual supplement of the 2004-09 policy was released for the year 2005-06 on April 8, 2005. The Supplement announced a number of policy initiatives. These include simplification of procedures, reduction in transaction cost, neutralization of incidence of levies and duties on inputs used for exports and development of global hubs for manufacturing, trading and services.

The study has been divided into two parts. While Part 'A' deals with India's trade during ancient, medieval and modern periods, Part 'B' deals with the contemporary period for which detailed figures are available from DGCI&S.

PART–A

1

Trade-Ancient India

Trade between India and the outside world has been going on from antiquity. India, rated as one of the oldest civilizations, was carrying on trade with the neighbouring East Asian, the West Asian and East African regions and China, its northern neighbour, since the earliest of times. It also had trade relations with other ancient civilizations, like Egypt, Mesopotamia (today's Iraq) and the Roman Empire. Trade with Europe followed and was of a much larger magnitude.

Several European and American scholars are now firmly of the view that India was carrying on maritime commerce since at least 3000 B.C. There are references in Chinese historical accounts of maritime traders 'bringing Typical Indian products to China as far back as 7th Century B.C. This is confirmed by Charles Verilinden, the honorary Chairman, International Commission for Maritime History, who says "We cannot exclude the possibility that China on the east and Africa on the west were both reached in the 7th century B.C. by Indian navigation." There is a possibility that Indians could have gone there even earlier.

"We talk today about globalism as if it were the latest thing, but trade was going on in antiquity at a scale and scope that is truly impressive," says Willeke, who made most of her contributions as a post-doctoral fellow at Leiden University in the Netherlands. "These people were taking incredible risks with their lives and fortune to make money."

Archaeologists from the UCLA and the University of Delaware have unearthed the most extensive remains to date for sea trade between Egypt and India and Europe during the Roman Empire, adding to mounting evidence that spices and other exotic cargo were traded with Europe over sea as well as land. "The silk route gets a lot of attention, but we have found a wealth of evidence indicating that sea trade between Egypt and India was also important for transporting exotic cargo and it may even have served as a link with the Far East," says Steve E. Sidebothern, a history professor at the University of Delaware.

Further, an international team of archaeologists, has excavated Berenike, a long abandoned Egyptian port on the Red Sea, near the border with Sudan. Among buried ruins of buildings that date back to Roman rule, the team discovered vast quantities of teak wood, indigenous to India and today's Myanmar, but not capable of growing in Egypt, Africa or Europe. The team found copper nails and metal sheeting, materials associated with ship-building activities.

That India was carrying on trade with West Asian and East African regions, which were the earliest trading nations, is generally accepted. What has not received the attention it deserves is the role of Arabs, who were the close compatriots of India in this trade. Their role relates to the "dim dawn" of civilization, says Dr. Baldeo Sahai in his book on Indian Shipping.

The earliest trade the Arabs had with India was in beautiful beads, ornaments, cloth, gems, resins, aromatic grasses, ivory, semi-precious stones and other articles. Very soon to their list of imports from India were added ginger, camphor, pepper and several other spices. Good timber, like teak and black wood, was also taken in large quantities for making ships. India's imports included copper, coral, topaz, antimony, tin, lead and a little wine and wheat.

Monsoon winds, rightly called trade winds, played a key role in the trade and commerce of the ancient east with other parts of the world. At a time when the sailing crafts were not mechanized and did not use steam or fossil fuel, the sailors depended on wind power of the south-east and north-east monsoons. The behaviour of monsoons was well known to sailors from India, Arabia and Persia since very early times and the mariners, who reached China in the Seventh Century BC, could not have feared sailing on the open seas.

Diggings at the ancient Egyptian port town of Berenike have produced spices and gem fragments that prove that Indian goods routinely made their way to Egypt. In particular, archaeologists found the largest single cache of black pepper from antiquity – 16 pounds-ever excavated. The team dates back the peppercorns, which were grown in southern India, during antiquity to 1st century. Peppercorns of the same vintage have been excavated in Germany. Spices used in Europe during antiquity may have passed through this port. In a dump that dates back to Roman times, the team also found Indian coconuts and 'batik' cloth as well as an array of material.

Along with the rest of Egypt, Berenike was controlled by the Roman Empire during the first and second centuries. During the same period, the overland route to Europe from India through Pakistan, Iran and Mesopotamia (today's Iraq) was controlled by adversaries of the Roman Empire, making overland routes difficult for Roman merchants.

Meanwhile, Roman texts that address the relative costs of different shipping methods describe overland transport as at least 20 times more expensive than sea trade.

"Overland transport was incredibly expensive, so whenever possible people in antiquity preferred shipping, which was vastly cheaper," says Sidebothern. Berenike is on the eastern side of Egypt and was in an ideal position to ship goods down the Red Sea and to Africa or Asia by sea or by land across Egypt to Alexandria, and from there to the rest of the Roman Empire.

Roman trade with India through the overland caravan routes via Anatolia and Persia, though at a relative trickle compared to later times, antedated the southern trade route via the Red Sea and Monsoons, which started around the beginning of the Common Era (CE) following the reign of Augustus and his conquest of Egypt. Having extended the Empires reach to the upper Nile, the Romans naturally encountered the great warrior trading nation of Axum (On the Red Sea, in todays Ethiopia) which had been trading with India and Egypt for several centuries.

Further, a contention that Buddhism encouraged and facilitated trade, has been made by Zinru Liu in her book "Ancient India and Ancient China, trade and religious exchanges AD1600." She says the trade was almost entirely in luxury goods, used for conspicuous consumption, to improve and maintain the position of the elite. She suggests that the consumption was by the emperors and aristocrats of China and India. She argues that the Chinese and Indian governments actively supported trade.

Historians have long believed that such trade between the two ancient civilizations existed, based on writings they have found in ancient books. The most recent archaeological find goes a long way towards cementing India's reputation as a major trade centre alongside China.

One of the major episodes of ancient Indian history was the march by Alexander the Great towards India in 332 BC. The political significance of Alexander's conquests was minimal, but the commercial consequences were of great importance. For the first time, the people of India came into direct contact on an extensive scale with a dynamic and comparatively younger European power. It had a far reaching impact on trade and commerce of the two peoples. The Arabs and the Jews no longer retained exclusive control over Indian trade.

If the Greeks provided a window to India, the Romans opened the flood gates of maritime trade. The trade expanded enormously and fresh items were added from time to time. The successive conquests of Mediterranean peoples had brought unprecedented treasures to Rome, which the Romans were able to spend to buy all exotic and tantalizingly tasty items of the orient. India was the main producer of these articles and profited enormously. The most important export items were pepper and pearls. Other articles from India included silk, fine textiles and saffron. Imports consisted of copper, coral, topaz and antimony.

The collapse of the Roman Empire adversely affected their trade with India and diverted the attention of the Indian merchants to new markets in South-East Asia and the Far East. But trade with West Asia continued as before. Thus, the western and the eastern coasts "were studded with ports throbbing with trade."

In the period after the birth of Christ, there is mention in Kautilyas Arthshastra, Brahad Samhita, the Mahabharata and the Ramayana of Kambojas being formidable warriors, besides being "excellent traders", agriculturists and cattle-culturists. Earliest literary sources from north India refer to Southerners, including Kambojas, Kashmiras and Gandharas, as being involved in trade on horses.

However, there is Buddhist reference to a trader named Bahyua, who was a native of Bharukachchs (modern Bharoch) in South-east Saurashtra (Gujarat). He engaged in trade, voyaging in a sea ship. He sailed down the river Indus across the sea seven times and returned home safe. On the eighth occasion, while on his way to Swarnabhoomi, his ship was wrecked and he floated ashore on a plank. This ancient Buddhist evidence verifies that trade ships plied regularly between the upper Indus towns of Kambhoja, Gandhara, Kashmira and sea ports of Bharukachche, Suparekhja and Swaranbhoomi.

Evidence exists that horse merchants from Kambhoja were in active trade with Eastern, Southern and Western India and as far as Ceylon. This trade has been going on as late as middle ages. King Devapale of Bengal (810-850 CE), King Vishnu Vardhene of Hoysala dynasty of Mysore (1106-1153 CE), and King Vallabhadeva of Pandya Kingdom (12th Century

CE) located in the extreme southern tip of India had powerful Kamboja horses in their cavalary.

It is now evident that trade between India and the outside world was being carried on as early as third century BC, if not earlier. The traders used both the land route and sea to carry on trade. Besides West Asia and Europe, India had trade with China and the neighbouring countries of East Asia.

2

Trade—Medieval India

During the medieval period, when the sultans and the Mughals ruled India, India's foreign trade expanded. The accounts of foreign travellers contain descriptions of a wide variety of exquisite goods sold in the markets of those days. India was famous for its textiles, which formed one of the chief items of export.

East Bengal was an important region for a wide variety of textiles. Ibn Batuta, the 14th century Moorish traveller, saw many cotton trade centres during his sojourn in Bengal. Silks were also manufactured there. The textile products included quilts of embroidered tussar, or munga, or cotton, or jute, silk and brocade-edged handkerchiefs. Dhaka muslin was renowned for its fineness. Kasim Bazaar in Bengal was an important trade centre for cotton and silk goods.

Sribund a type of cloth used for tying turbans was manufactured in Bengal. It was highly popular. Duarte Barbosa a Portuguese official in Cochin in the early 16th century described Surat in Gujarat, in the western region, as a leading cotton trade centre. Textiles from Gujarat were exported to Arab countries and to South-east Asia. Patola, which is a kind of silk, dyed in natural colours was highly Popular in South-east Asia. It was very much in demand among the wealthy classes in Malaya, Indonesia, and the Philippines. Similarly, Malabar in Kerala was famous for its coloured printed cloth material. The other important textiles producing centres in the south were Golconda, Shaliat and Pulicat. The last two were major trading centres for a wide variety of cottons. Golconda was famous for its Kalamkaaris.

These were finely painted cotton fabrics with motifs from the Hindu mythology. They were exported through the port city of Masulipatnam.

Palampores, which were another variety of painted fabrics, were popular in the Mughal and Deccan courts. These were bedspreads made of Calico cloth. The borders of these pieces were block printed, while the centre depicted the 'Tree of Life' motif made by hand. Indian textiles whether from Bengal, Gujarat or the South were highly appreciated abroad for their fine texture, elaborate design and brilliant colours.

Hardwood furniture, embellished with inlay work was a very popular item. The furniture was modelled on the European design, but the expensive carvings and inlays were inspired by the ornate Mughal style. The production centres were in Sindh, Gujarat and the Deccan. Mother-of-pearl inlay against a black lac background was a traditional design in Gujarat.

Carpets were used both in ancient and medieval India, but it was in the 16th century during the Mughal era that the skill of carpet weaving touched new heights. It had become an important profession by then and all the major courts of the country encouraged it. Carpets produced during the Mughal era depicted either animals in combat or flowers. The flowers were woven so meticulously that they could be easily identified. The affinity of the Great Mughals with nature is evident from the designs of carpets made during these times. Many varieties of ornamental work in cut stones, ivory, pearl and tortoise shells were produced in South India. Pearl fishing was a major industry there. Diamonds were procured from the Deccan, while sapphires and rubies were imported from Pegu in Myanmar and Ceylon. Major centres were established in Puliat, Calicut and Vijayanagar for cutting and polishing these stones.

Indian arts and crafts were patronised by Indian rulers. They were unmatched for their beauty and skill and were popular in European countries. During the Mughal era, the

European traders used to employ local artisans at the manufacturing centres setup by them at various places in India.

India's exports far exceeded her imports, both in the number of items as well as in volume. The chief items of imports were horses from Kabul and Arabia, dried fruits and precious stones. India also imported glassware from Europe, high grade textiles like satin from West Asia, while China supplied raw silk and porcelain. Foreign luxury goods were highly popular among the royalty and the nobility. These included wines, dried fruits, precious stones, corals, scented oils, perfumes and velvets.

During the Sultanate period, articles of everyday use, as well as luxury articles were exported to Syria, Arabia and Persia from Bengal and Cambay. These included silks, gold-embroidered cloth caps, exquisitely-designed clay pots and pans, guns, knives and scissors. The other articles of export were sugar, indigo, oils, ivory, sandal wood, spices, diamonds and other precious gems and coconut. Arab traders shipped Indian goods to European countries through the Red Sea and the Mediterranean ports. Indian products were also sent to East Africa, Malaya, China and the Far East. In China, Indian textiles were valued more than silk. Trade was also conducted through overland routes with Afghanistan, Central Asia and Persia. The route lay through Kashmir, Quetta and the Khyber Pass. Iraq and Bukhara were the other areas with which India conducted trade via the land route.

Foreign trade was in the hands of both local and foreign merchants. Many European travellers had settled in the coastal regions. Limbodar in Gujarat was a major exporting centre. Horses imported from Arabia were sent from the port of Bhatkal in Goa to the southern kingdoms. The traders of Malabar, Gujarat and foreign settlers controlled business in the port cities of Calicut, Khambat, and Mangalore. Chinese ships docked at Quilon and Calicut, while in Khambat the volume of trade was such that 3000 ships visited this port annually. This gives an idea of the magnitude of India's foreign trade.

Trade with China and South-east Asia was mainly carried on through the port of Sonargaon now known as Dacca. Vijaynagar, which was the richest and most expensive state in the 15th and 16th centuries, enjoyed the most voluminous maritime trade with diverse countries such as Persia, Arabia, Africa, the Malayan Archipelago, Burma, China and the numerous islands in the Indian Ocean. The magnitude of trade can be surmised from the fact that there were 300 ports to facilitate the movement of goods. Shipbuilding flourished in coastal towns.

The city of Vijaynagar was a teeming market place for both exports and imports. The fabulous wealth of the Empire left the foreigners dumbfounded. The people, irrespective of strata of society they belonged to, possessed vast quantities of gold, diamonds and material wealth. Domingo Paes described the citizens as being heavily bejewelled. Abdur Razzak, the Khurasani ambassador to the court of Vijaynagar, refers to the treasury which had chambers filled with molten gold. The Gujarati and Marwari businessmen who controlled trade between the coastal towns and North India were extremely wealthy and spent large sums on the construction of temples. The Multanis, who were Hindus and the Khurasanis who were Muslims, controlled the trade with Central and Western Asia. Many of these Multanis and Khurasanis settled in Delhi, where they lived luxurious lives. Cambay was also home to an affluent mercantile community.

India enjoyed a favourable balance in trade relations with other countries during this period. Her earnings from the export of textiles, sugar, spices and indigo alone went up to crores of rupees (a crore is 10 million). The state coffers were amply stocked with gold and silver to pay for the import of luxury goods they enjoyed.

3

Trade—Modern India

The modern era begins with the arrival of the Europeans in the last decade of the 15th century after the visit of Vasco da Gama in 1498. The Portuguese, followed by the Dutch traders and later by the British traders entered India. The battle of Plassy in 1757 entrenched the British firmly in India. The East India Company had monopoly of Indo-British trade. The monopoly was abolished in 1830, largely due to growing pressures from Britain's industrial capitalists and private traders. In 1833, the company ceased to be a trading concern altogether.

India's foreign trade during this period, comprised India's export of textiles, food grains, metal wares, spices, etc. while, its imports consisted of precious metals and some manufactured goods. The commodity composition of the trade started changing with the impact of the Industrial Revolution, which resulted in larger production of manufactured goods in volumes for which the British market was inadequate and which led to increased demand for raw materials. The East India Company, which turned into the country's rulers used public revenues for the purchase of goods in India for export purposes.

Bipan Chandra says in his book, The Rise and Growth of Economic Nationalism in India: "In the 19th century, specially after 1850, India took big strides forward in its foreign trade, which virtually ushered in a commercial revolution in the country. Imports and exports increased considerably in both volume and value; they also underwent dramatic changes in their scope and character."

Chandra adds "While prior to 1813, and ever since remote antiquity, India had primarily been an exporter of manufactures and importer of precious metals and luxury products, it gradually became, particularly after 1858, an exporter of agricultural raw materials and food grains and importer of manufactured products. Cotton and silk textiles and other traditional items of export were gradually replaced by a variety of agricultural products, chief of them being raw cotton and jute, tea and coffee, opium, oil seeds and wheat and rice, the last two constituting 17 and 26 per cent of total exports in 1881-2 and 1904-5 respectively. Among imports, cotton yarns and cloth, metals, machinery, sugar and oil began to dominate, cotton products alone constituting 24 and 39 per cent of total imports in 1881-2 and 1904-5 respectively."

"The second half of 19th century", says Chandra "witnessed the emergence of a new trend in the foreign trade of India. On the one had, iron and steel, machinery and mill work started entering the country in steadily increasing quantities; on the other, exports of cotton and jute textiles, now as products of modern machines, began once again to find their way into export trade and to steadily assume growing importance."

Over the years, both the volume and the composition of India's trade changed. Girish Mishra in his book on economic history of modern India, quotes K.N. Choudhuri in his book, the Economic Development of India under the East India Company, as saying "Between 1814 and 1848, the volume and value of India's exports and imports more than quadrupled." During 1814-1857, there was a rapid increase in India's foreign trade. The value of exports increased from Rs. 68.3 million to Rs. 183 million between 1814-15 and 1854-55. The value of imports grew even more rapidly from Rs. 11.9 million to Rs. 174 million.

Regarding the composition of trade, in the first half of 19th century, it had undergone a transformation of exports into the category of primary commodities with corresponding increase of manufactured goods in its imports. In 1814, exports comprised indigo (an industrial dye), textiles, raw silk, cotton, opium, sugar, etc. By 1857-58, the share of indigo declined from 20 per cent of total in 1814-15 to 6.1 per cent and of textiles from 14.3 per cent to 2.9 per cent. On the other hand, the relative shares of cotton, opium, raw materials, etc increased, says Girish Mishra. "The manufacturing and commercial interest in Britain were beginning to be aware of India's position as a supplier of raw material and the advantages that accrued from it to the home industries," Mishra quotes Chaudhuri as saying.

During the period, India's major trade partners were Britain and China (Britain accounting for half and China almost one-fourth). The rest of the trade turnover was shared by Persian Gulf region, France, Malay, USA, Burma, Indonesia and a host of other countries.

After India's administration was taken over by the British Crown in 1858, an altogether new phase began in the history of India's foreign trade, says Mishra. "A significant feature of this phase was the continuous increase in the value of trade turnover." During 1858-93, India's foreign trade increased rapidly, aided as it was by the development of transport and communications — the opening up of the Suez Canal, which reduced the distance between India and Europe by four to five thousand miles, resulting in reduction in shipping charges—restoration of peace and order after take-over by the Crown. The average value of India's imports increased from Rs. 410 million per year in 1869-70 — 1870-74 to Rs. 890 million during 1889-90 – 1893-94, an increase of 115 per cent. During the same period, the average annual value of exports went up from Rs. 580 million to Rs. 1,090 million, rising by 88 per cent.

However, the last six years of the century, beginning 1894-95 saw stagnation in India's exports. The average annual value of India's merchandise imports declined to Rs.750 million and that of exports to Rs. 1,070 million, following natural calamities, like famine, plague and earthquake, as also war between China and Japan, which affected India's exports to China. However, throughout the period, India enjoyed trade surplus of as much as Rs. 200 million to Rs. 400 million. The export surplus, however, did not give any real benefit to India as most of it went out to pay for invisibles, which included services of British military and civil personnel, technical know-how and payment to traders, bankers and a host of entrepreneurs.

In the first 13 years of the 20th century, there was rapid expansion of India's foreign trade. Says Mishra "As the world entered the twentieth century, it experienced unprecedented and widespread prosperity. Internally, agricultural production was better and the peasantry experienced an increase in their purchasing power." These conditions continued up to 1907-08. In that year, both the exports and imports were higher by 70 per cent as compared to their level in 1990-91. "Although in 1908-09 there was a setback to the upward trend in India's foreign trade, the decade rate of growth for both exports and imports during 1901-02 – 1910-11 exceeded all 19th century rates, except for 1850s."

There was, however, a big change in the composition of India's exports and imports. During this period, India's cotton textile industry came into being and piece goods were completely eliminated from India's export items. During the second half of the 19th century, food grains, jute, oilseeds, tea, hides and skins and cotton textiles became very important items in India's exports, as against indigo, raw silk, opium and cotton in the first half.

There was substantial spurt in India's export trade in food grains during the second half of the 19th century and up to the beginning of the First World War. Food grains accounted for 10 to 20 per cent of total value of India's exports. In 1891-92 and 1904-05, they accounted for more than one-fourth.

With the opening of the Suez Canal and the introduction of fast-moving steam ships, food grains could be exported without any risk of deterioration in quality. Raw jute and jute goods were among items whose exports increased rapidly. The USA and Australia were the main markets for these products. As a result of free trade policy being pursued by India, a range of manufactured goods entered India.

The Two World Wars

The period from 1914 to 1945 was marked by two World Wars, excepting the period 1920-38 – the inter-war years. The wars adversely affected India's foreign trade. Trade with 'enemy countries,' like Germany in both the wars and Japan in the case of Second World War experienced complete stoppage. There was virtual stoppage of trade with the Russian Empire during World War I because of difficulties of transportation. Trade even with neutral countries was restricted. Normal trade channels got disrupted and shipping became a real problem because of increasing risks on high seas and rising trade and demurrage charges.

Though in value terms imports and exports increased or compared favourably to the period prior to the First World War, there appeared to be considerable shrinkage in volume terms. The average annual value of imports during the first World War came to Rs. 1,556.0 million, while those of exports to Rs. 2,242.3 million. The figures for pre-war years were Rs. 2,261.00 million and Rs. 2,242.00 million. The volume of imports, however, showed a decline by 50 per cent and exports by 25 per cent. The main reason for this, according to Mishra was sharp increase in import prices, while export prices were not allowed to increase as they were controlled by the government. Terms of trade, thus, moved against India. Yet during the war, India enjoyed a trade surplus of Rs. 715.00 million in spite of the fact that its trade relations with a number of countries got terminated and terms of trade went against it.

As stated above, the war reversed the change in the direction of trade, witnessed up to 1913. Almost complete stoppage of trade with enemy countries, virtual stoppage of trade with certain allies, like Russian Empire, because of difficulties in transportation, restriction of trade relations even with neutral countries and insurmountable problems created by lack of shipping facilities and trouble-free passage affected the direction of trade.

The share of Britain and British Empire in India's exports increased from 24 per cent and 41 per cent respectively in 1914 to 28 and 52 per cent respectively in 1919. 'The share of continental Europe declined and Germany, which took 10 per cent of India's exports before the war was eliminated and this hit Indian agriculture hard. Japan and the USA improved their share in India's exports from 9 per cent each in 1914 to 12 per cent and 13 per cent respectively in 1919.

The share of the U.K. and continental Europe in India's imports was reduced considerably. Germany contributing 6.4 per cent to the country's imports in 1914 was eliminated. The UK contributed only 46 per cent to India's imports in 1919 as against 64 per cent in 1914 due to her being busy in war production, but still remained her principal supplier. The USA and Japan concentrated on Indian markets and improved their share from 2.6 per cent and 20 per cent respectively in 1919. Japan made her inroads in textiles and the USA in metallurgical industries. The proportion of manufactured goods in exports increased from 23.6 per cent, the pre-war average, to 32.1 per cent during the war and in imports it declined from 76.6 per cent to 73.4 per cent.

During the Second World War, there was an increase in the value of both imports and exports up to 1941-42. The value of imports went up from Rs. 1,523.7 million in 1938-39 to Rs. 1,652.9 million in 1939-40 and Rs. 1,731.4 million in 1941-42. There was, however, some setback in 1940-41 when it declined to Rs. 1,569.7 million. The value of exports fluctuated throughout the Second World War. It rose from Rs. 1,692.1 million in 1938-39 to Rs. 2,135.7 million in 1939-40 and declined to Rs.1,987 million in 1940-41, to rise again to Rs. 2,528.9 million in 1941-42. It went down to Rs. 1,949.7 million in 1942-43. During the last two years of the war, it rose, reaching Rs. 2,108.4 million in 1943-44 and Rs. 2,273.3 million in 1944-45.

As during the First World War, while the recorded value of imports and exports in 1944-45 stood at 34 per cent and 35 per cent respectively over that in 1938-39, there was a heavy decline in the quantum of India's foreign trade. While the quantum of exports in 1944-45 was 53 per cent of that in 1938-39, the quantum of imports stood at only 40 per cent in 1943-44, but improved to 71 per cent in 1944-45 due to heavy imports in that year. The balance of trade remained throughout in India's favour. In 1943-44, it recorded Rs. 930.7 million, the highest for 20 years. It was 45.3 per cent more than the pre-war level.

Inter-war Years 1920-38

Increased world demand for raw materials and the disappearance of war time difficulties and restrictions led to a big spurt in India's exports, which crossed Rs. 3,360 million mark in 1919-20, while imports aggregated to Rs. 2,217.9 million. The trade surplus was around Rs. 1,143 million. The next year, however, the situation changed and imports exceeded exports and there was a deficit in the balance of trade to the tune of Rs. 798 million with imports going up to Rs. 3,475.6 million and exports coming down to Rs. 2,677 million. The increase in imports was in view of accumulated unsatisfied demand during the war years.

The imports came down in subsequent years following the boycott of foreign goods launched by the Indian National Congress. Exports, however, increased and there was a surplus in the trade balance to the tune of Rs. 698.8 million in 1922-23. During the following three years, there was a rapid rise in India's exports, which crossed Rs. 4,000 million mark.

After 1924-25, there was a decline in the value of India's exports, which went down from Rs. 4,002.4 million to Rs. 3,868.2 million in 1925-26, further to Rs. 3,110.5 million in 1926-27, increasing to Rs. 3,302.6 million in 1927-28 and Rs. 3,395 million in 1928-29. Although there was a decline in exports in value terms compared to 1925-26, in volume terms exports increased, which meant that per unit realization was going down.

Thus, the terms of trade moved against India. India's export surplus, which was Rs. 1,510 million in 1925-26, declined to Rs. 702.3 million in 1926-27 and further to Rs. 687.3 million in 1927-28.

The 1920s closed with a severe setback to India's foreign trade. The Great Depression (1929-33) was an era of worldwide slump. India's foreign trade in 1932-33 in value terms was less than 50 per cent of what it was in 1929-30. The decline was sudden and continuous for four long years. The trade surplus came down to Rs. 10 million.

The impact of Great Depression began subsiding from 1933. As business activities revived in the West, India's exports increased. The value of exports rose from Rs. 1,360 million in 1932-33 to Rs.2,020 million in 1936-37. As the signs of coming world war began to appear, stockpiling of raw material and rearmament started. It meant increasing exports for India.

Imports did not increase because of increasing domestic production of manufactures. The value of imports declined from Rs. 2,497.1 million in 1929.39 to Rs. 1,277.2 million in 1936-37. The balance of trade became favourable and there was a surplus of Rs. 746.7 million in 1936-37. There was, however, the separation of Burma (Myanmar) from India in 1937, which adversely affected India's exports of rice and timber.

There was a significant change in the composition of India's trade, which in effect reflected the changing character of the Indian economy since 1920. There was a continuous increase in the proportion of raw material in India's total imports while there was a continuous decline in the proportion of manufactured goods during the period 1920-21 to 1939-40.

The proportion of food, drink and tobacco in India's imports remained more or less constant. The proportion of raw materials and capital goods to total imports increased from 38.8 per cent in 1925-26 to 54.3 per cent in 1938-39, while the relative share of consumer goods declined from 54 per cent to 33 per cent during the same period because of their increased availability in the country.

So far as exports are concerned, the share of raw materials went down and that of manufactured goods increased slightly. There was a diversion of raw materials to meet the growing demand of newly-established industries in India. In 1938-39, 46 per cent of India's exports were accounted for by jute manufactures, raw cotton and tea and 30 per cent by raw jute, oil seeds, grains, pulses, cotton manufactures, processed hides and skin, etc.

The direction of India's foreign trade also underwent a change. The importance of British Empire as the source of India's imports went down from 75 per cent in pre-war years to 65 per cent in post –war period. It was 54 per cent in 1928-29 and 45 per cent in 1931-32. Britain alone had supplied 65 per cent of India's imports in pre-war years, but in 1931-32, it accounted for only 35.5 per cent of India's imports. Notwithstanding the adoption of Imperial Preference, India drew more and more of its imports from the USA, Japan and Germany. The share of Germany in India's imports went up from 6 per cent in pre-war years to 8.1 per cent in post war years. Similarly, the share of Japan and the USA went up from 3 per cent each to 10.6 and 10.2 per cent respectively.

The adoption of Imperial Preference in 1932 led to an increase in the share of the British Empire from 45 per cent in 1931-32 to 58 per cent in 1938-39. However, the share of the UK declined to 31 per cent in 1938-39.

So far as exports are concerned, the share of British Empire went down from 41 per cent in pre-war years to around 35 per cent in 1928-29. However, by 1938-39, it increased to 54 per cent. Following the adoption of Imperial Preference, Britain's share rose from 25 per cent in pre-war years to 34 per cent in 1938-39. The share of Japan and the USA was at its highest in the post World War period at 13 per cent and 12 per cent respectively, but declined to 9 per cent and 8 per cent respectively in 1938-39. The share of Germany, was 9.7 per cent in 1928-29, but declined to 5 per cent in 1938-39.

By the end of this period, India's trade with British Empire was balanced, but India's heavy trade surplus with countries outside the British Empire was reduced considerably from Rs.1,000 million in 1913-14 to Rs.160 million in 1938-39.

At the end of the Second World War, there was a spurt in India's foreign trade. The value of imports went up from Rs. 2,921.5 million in 1945-46 to Rs. 3,303.1 million in 1946-47 and further to Rs. 4,458.8 million in 1947-48. The value of exports rose from Rs. 2,663.9 million to Rs. 3,203.4 million and then to Rs. 4,082.4 million. The balance of trade showed a deficit, which rose from Rs. 257.6 million in 1945-46 to Rs. 376.4 million in 1947-48.

The partition of the country had an adverse impact on India's foreign trade. Exports, which were of the order of Rs. 4,850 million in 1949-50 went up to Rs. 6,060 million in 1950-51 and further to Rs. 7,160 million in 1951-52, but declined to Rs. 5,780 million in 1952-53 and further to Rs. 5,310 million in 1953-54. The trend of exports going up and down continued till 1966-87, when the upward trend started and there was no looking back. Exports went up to Rs. 16,080 million in 1971-72.

Nevertheless, there was constant decline in the percentage of India's exports when compared to world exports. India's exports declined from 2.6 per cent of world exports in 1948 to 0.72 per cent of world exports in 1970. Taking note of this the "Medium-term Export, Strategy, 2002-07," released in 2002 stressed the urgent need to raise the share of India's exports to one per cent of world exports in five year. This was achieved in 2005, two years ahead of the schedule. India needs to maintain the tempo by realizing the growth potential of each item and exploiting the demand of each country and region. A commodity-wise and country-wise study, thus, assumes importance.

PART–B : INDIA'S TRADE; CONTEMPORARY PERIOD (1960-61 TO 2009-10)

4

Trade Policy and WTO

For India, foreign trade policy is of recent origin. On the eve of Independence in 1947, foreign trade of India was typical of a colonial economy. Trade relations were mainly confined to Britain and other Commonwealth countries. Exports consisted chiefly of raw materials and plantation crops while imports composed of light consumer goods and other manufactures.

Prior to 1990, India followed a policy of import liberalization through a combination of high tariffs and quantitative controls, which led to a bias against exports. The strategy was 'inward looking,' which relied on encouraging domestic production for domestic market. As Dr. Bimal Jalan in his book, 'The Indian economy problems and prospects' points out: "The impact of import liberalization in generating higher inputs for domestic use is likely to occur immediately, while the favourable impact on exports will occur after some time. In the meantime, the balance of payments crisis may deepen."

So far as exports are concerned, Dr. Jalan says that the period up to 1972-73 was one of 'extreme export pessimism.' During the period, planners believed that the terms of trade of developing countries were destined to deteriorate over time regardless of the policies of developing countries. This, says Dr. Jalan "was a crucial assumption as it firmly established a case for discouragement of exports and for policies which encouraged production for the domestic market."

In the period between 1973, when the oil crisis took place, and 1983, exports were accorded a high priority. In the mid-1970s, a number of changes were made in industrial and trade policies, which provided special treatment to exports. Thus, for example, it was provided that industrial capacity used for exports was not to be counted as part of licensed capacity. Simplified procedures were also introduced in import of technology, raw materials and capital goods for exports. Export Processing Zones (EPZs) were established and promotional agencies set up to promote exports. Financial incentives for exports were enhanced and exchange rate policies were used in support of exports.

In the period beginning 1983, exports were seen as an integral part of industrial and development policy. The policy emphasized on measures 'essential' for export promotion, such as technological up-gradation, increase in size of plants, freer imports and domestic and international competition for the entire industrial sector. After stagnation in the first half of the eighties, export growth picked up after 1985-86.

Over the years, trade policy has undergone fundamental shifts to correct the earlier anti-export bias through the withdrawal of quantitative restrictions (QRs), reduction and rationalization of tariffs, liberalization in trade and payments regime and improved access to export incentives, besides a realistic and market-based exchange rate. In early 2002, the Government presented a Medium Term Export Strategy (MTES) for 2002-2007 providing a vision for creating a stable policy environment with indicative sector-wise targets, with a mission to achieve one per cent of global trade by 2007.

This was followed by a new Export and Import (EXIM) Policy, announced on March 31, 2002. The EXIM Policy sought to usher in an environment free of restrictions and controls. The policy, which was soon to be replaced by Foreign Trade Policy 2004-09 and later by FTP 2009-14, sought to strengthen SEZ, provide a package of incentives for small scale, cottage and handicrafts sector, including exemption from maintaining the average export obligation under the Export Promotion Capital Goods Scheme (EPCG) and sought to focus on measures to encourage value-added exports in the garment sector.

Policy measures announced in the Union Budget 2002-03 included a comprehensive package for the development of Special Economic Zones, including entitlement of these Zones to procure duty free equipment, raw materials, components, etc whether imported or purchased locally.

Overall, during the last 60 years, India's foreign trade has undergone a complete change in terms of composition and direction. Exports cover a wide range of traditional and non-traditional items while imports consist mainly of capital goods, petroleum products, raw materials and chemicals to meet the ever-increasing needs of a developing and diversifying economy. For about 40 years (1950-90), foreign trade of India suffered from strict bureaucratic and discretionary controls.

Till early 1990s, India was a closed economy. Average tariff exceeded 200 per cent and QRs were extensive. Since 1990, trade reforms have produced remarkable results. Average non-agricultural tariffs have fallen below 15 per cent. Quantitative restrictions on imports have been eliminated. India, however, retains its right to protect its agriculture or industry when need be. Agricultural tariffs averaged between 30 and 40 per cent. Anti-dumping measures have been liberally used to protect trade.

As mentioned above, India unveiled on August 31, 2004, a new foreign trade policy (FTP) for the period 2004-09, which sought to achieve two major objectives — firstly of doubling India's share of global merchandise trade by 2009 and secondly of using trade policy as an effective instrument of economic growth with a thrust on employment generation.

Further, on 27th August, 2009, Foreign Trade Policy 2009-14, was unveiled, the main features of which include continuation of Duty Exemption Pass Book (DEPB) Scheme, and zero duty "Export Promotion Capital Goods (EPCG)

Scheme, rationalization of additional export obligation under EPCG, provision of additional markets under Focus Market Scheme and additional products under Focus Products Schemes.

The FTP 2004 identified certain thrust sectors having prospects for export expansion and potential for employment generation. These sectors include agriculture, handlooms and handicrafts, gems and jewelry and leather and footwear sectors. Key strategies to achieve these objectives ***inter alia*** *include unshackling of controls and creating an atmosphere of trust and transparency, simplifying procedures and bringing down transaction costs.*

The strategies also include neutralizing incidence of all levies on inputs used in products meant for export, facilitating development of India as a global hub for manufacturing, trading and services, identifying and nurturing special focus areas to generate additional employment opportunities, particularly in semi-urban and rural areas. Facilitating technological and infrastructural upgradation of the Indian economy, specially through the import of capital goods and equipment, avoiding inverted duty, structure and ensuring that domestic sectors are not disadvantaged in trade agreements formed as part of the strategy, which also included upgrading of infrastructural network related to the entire foreign trade chain to international standards and further revitalizing the Board of Trade by redefining its role and inducting into it experts on trade policy and to involve Indian embassies as key players.

A new scheme to accelerate growth of exports, called Target Plus was introduced in the FTP. Under the scheme, exporters achieving a quantum growth in exports are entitled to duty free credit based on incremental exports, substantially higher than the actual export target fixed.

The policy also aimed at unshackling controls and creating an atmosphere of trust and transparency by bringing down transaction costs and identifying and nurturing focus areas to develop India as a global hub for manufacturing, trading and services.

Trade policy reforms with their focus on liberalization, openness, transparency and globalization, have provided an export friendly atmosphere with simplified procedure for trade facilitation.

The FTP 2004 further improved upon the Export Production Capital Goods (EPCG) scheme. Import of second hand capital goods without any restriction on age has been permitted and minimum depreciated value of plant and machinery to be relocated into India has been reduced from Rs. 500 million to Rs. 250 million.

The Union Budget 2004-05 reiterated the policy approach of lowering customs duties in a measured way to align India's tariff structure to ASEAN countries. The Budget underlined the need for a special fiscal and regulatory regime for the Special Economic Zones (SEZ), given their role as growth engines that can boost manufacturing and exports. Towards this end, a bill for regulating SEZs, to make India a major hub for manufacturing and exports was proposed.

Other proposals announced in the Budget included identification of 85 items to be taken out from the SSI reservation list to provide space to these units to grow into medium enterprises. It also included a proposal to set up a fund for regeneration of traditional employment industries for the development of their export potential. The industries included coir, handloom, handicrafts, sericulture, leather, pottery and other cottage industries.

The annual supplement to the FTP, announced in April 2005, incorporated additional policy initiatives and further simplified the procedures. Moreover, a number of measures were announced in the annual supplement to the policy in April 2006 to achieve the objective of making India a gem and jewelry hub (details are given in the gem and jewelry sub-heading in the chapter on manufactured goods).

India is now aggressively pushing for a more liberal global trade regime, specially in services. It has assumed a leadership role among developing nations in global trade negotiations and played a critical part in Doha negotiations of the World Trade Organization (WTO), successor to General Agreement on Tariff and Trade.

By way of a background, it may be mentioned that the General Agreement on Tariffs and Trade (GATT), which was signed in 1947, was a multilateral agreement regulating trade among about 150 countries. According to its preamble, the purpose of the GATT was "substantial reduction of tariffs and other trade barriers and the elimination of preferences, on a reciprocal and mutually advantageous basis."

There have been eight rounds of negotiations addressing various trade issues. The most recent, the Uruguay Round, addressed issues such as tariffs, services, and the trade related aspects of intellectual property and investment measures.

The Uruguay Round, which was completed on December 15, 1993 after seven years of negotiations, resulted in an agreement among 117 countries (including the U.S.) to reduce trade barriers and to create more comprehensive and enforceable world trade rules. The agreement coming out of this round, 'The Final Act Embodying the Results of the Uruguay Round of Multilateral Trade Negotiations,' was signed in April 1994. This agreement also created the World Trade Organization (WTO), which came into being on January 1, 1995. The WTO implements the agreement, provides a forum for negotiating additional reductions of trade barriers and for settling policy disputes, and enforces trade rules.

India took upon itself the role of leader of the Group of 77 developing countries that lobbied hard and strong throughout the 1960s, 1970s, 1980s, and even some of the 1990s, to preserve the right to protect its economy through tariffs and quotas.

The issues, which India has taken up at WTO include trade in agriculture and negotiations in services, which include dental and health services, audio-visual services, tourism services, architectural services, computer aided services and maritime services.

Among services, an important service, being negotiated is movement of natural persons. While General Agreement on Trade in Services (GATS) recognizes movement of persons as one of the modes of supply of service, the emphasis by India for commitment by developed countries under this mode would correct an important imbalance and increase developing countries' participation in trade in services.

Under Trade Related Intellectual Property Rights (TRIPS), India has proposed that the multilateral register should be extended to products other than wines and spirit. Further as regards negotiations in public health, India maintains its position that the scope and the definition of diseases should not be diluted to infectious diseases as desired by some countries like the USA.

The Doha round of trade negotiations got a boost with members agreeing at Cancun on August 1 2004 to adopt a Framework Agreement, outlining the elements and principles, which will guide further negotiations. Similarly, the Doha Round got a fillip with a Ministerial Declaration adopted at the end of the conference in Hong Kong in December 2005.

Another ministerial declaration in Geneva on May 20, 1998, this time on global electronic-commerce, which had added a new dimension to trade policy, directed the WTO General Council to establish a comprehensive work programme to examine all trade related issues arising from electronic commerce.

The Framework Agreement explicitly agreed to eliminate export subsidies by a credible end date. The Framework also recognized the critical importance of agriculture to economic development of developing countries and the need to enable them to pursue agricultural policies that are supportive of their development goals, poverty reduction strategies, food security and livelihood concerns.

In the Ministerial Declaration, adopted at Hong Kong, it has been agreed that development programmes of developing countries that have minimal distorting effect will be incorporated into the green box. It has further been agreed that the three heaviest subsidizers, namely, the EU, the US and Japan, will attract the highest levels of cuts in their trade-distorting domestic support entitlements and that these cuts must be effective.

It has also been agreed that developing countries, like India will continue to have the right to provide marketing and transport subsidies on exports for five years beyond the end date for elimination of all forms of export subsidies. Further, the Hong Kong Ministerial Declaration has addressed some of the concerns of India in the movement of natural persons. For example, India has been pushing for the removal of Economic Needs Test, clear prescription of duration of stay, etc. It had often been noticed that domestic regulations created barriers for India's service providers even when the trading partners have made firm commitments.

While continuing with multilateral trade negotiations under WTO, India has been concluding Regional and Preferential trading agreements (RTAs), moving in some cases to Comprehensive Economic Cooperation Agreements (CECAs). Thus, a Framework Agreement on Comprehensive Economic Cooperation between ASEAN and India was signed by the Prime Minister of India and heads of governments of ASEAN countries on October 8, 2003 in Bali, Indonesia. An agreement on Trade in Goods was signed on August 13, 2009. The Agreement came into effect on January 1, 2010. The Agreement provides, among others, for elimination of basic customs duty on 80 per cent of tariff lines, accounting for 75 per cent trade in a gradual manner.

An India-South Korea comprehensive Partnership Agreement (CEPA) was signed on August 7, 2009. The Agreement covers trade in goods, investments and services and bilateral cooperation in areas of common interest. Under

CEPA, tariff will be reduced or eliminated in 93 per cent of Korea's tariff lines and 80 per cent of India's tariff lines.

Under negotiations are India-EU Trade and Investment Agreement, India-UK Economic and Financial dialogue, Framework Agreement on BIMSTEC (Bay of Bengal Multi-sectoral Technical and Economic Cooperation) FTA; Asia Pacific Trade agreement; India-Chile Framework Agreement on Economic Cooperation and PTA (Preferential Trading Agreement)/CECPA between India and Mauritius.

Thus, India has followed a trade policy, which while seeking to promote its exports, has at the same time championed the cause of other developing countries. India has, in this manner, sought to play a leadership role, which would inevitably help promote its exports.

5
Agriculture and Allied Products—Perishable

India, the second largest producer of fruits and vegetables in the world, is a major exporter of perishable fresh food items, which besides these two items, include meat and preparations, marine products and dairy and poultry products. India is also an exporter of floriculture products, which is a non-food perishable item. Nevertheless, although exports of fruits and vegetables, as also other items have received phenomenal growth in recent years, the growth is much below the potential, lacking as the country does in infrastructural support. India is also an importer of milk and cream.

Fruits and Vegetables

With an annual production of 94 million tons, India has the distinction of producing almost all tropical and exotic fruits and vegetables, helped as it is by its varied climatic conditions. However, due to the short shelf-life of these crops, as much as 30-35 per cent of fruits and vegetables perish during harvest, storage, grading, transport, packaging and distribution. There is the need for refrigerated transportation infrastructure and cold storage chains if the exports of fresh fruits and vegetables and other perishable agricultural items are to grow commensurate with India's capacity.

Fresh fruits and vegetables are two perishable items whose exports from India have been growing. The exports of fresh fruits and vegetables (Onions and other fresh vegetables, mangoes, grapes and other fruits) have nearly doubled in 2005-06 to Rs. 15,822 million from Rs. 8,696.3 million in

2000-01. In the next three years, the exports of fresh fruits, vegetables went up further to Rs. 36,379.11 million in 2008-09.

The growth over the decades has been phenomenal considering that exports of fresh fruits, vegetables and pulses were a mere Rs. 60 million in 1960-61. Malaysia, UAE, the UK, Bangladesh and Saudi Arabia are India's major markets for fresh fruits and vegetables. However, in a scenario, where India's overall exports have received a 24.58 per cent spurt in 2004-05, exports of fresh fruits and vegetables show a decline of 10.8 per cent to Rs. 13,637.10 million from Rs. 14,572.6 million in 2003-04, according to figures available from Agricultural and Processed Food Products Export Development Authority (APEDA).

A whopping growth of 97 per cent in the export of onions in 2003-04 over the previous year, which could not be maintained in the subsequent years, did the damage in bringing down the overall tally in the export of fruits and vegetables drastically in 2004-05, as all items except grapes showed marginal decline.

There is a story behind onion exports picking up, declining and then picking up again. India is the largest producer and a major exporter of onions. Exports were suspended from October 12, 1998 due to the steep rise in domestic prices. They were later allowed through designated canalizing agencies under a quota regime, but by then India had lost its traditional export market. In the course of years, the country has again picked up the market. Malaysia, Bangladesh, Sri Lanka, UAE and Singapore are India's major markets for onions.

Besides onion, vegetables exported by India include fresh potatoes, which go mainly to Germany, Italy, Sri Lanka, Mauritius and Nepal. Other vegetables exported are tomatoes, cauliflowers, cabbage, lettuce, lettuce fresh, carrots and turnips, radishes, beetroot fresh, cucumbers and gherkin fresh, peas, beans, asparagus fresh, mushrooms fresh, green chilly, plantain (curry banana) pumpkins, green pepper fresh/chilled and mixed vegetables. Most of them went in smaller quantities and to fewer countries.

Like onions, fresh potato is a major item of export. Uttar Pradesh, the largest producer of potatoes in India, is now exporting it in a big way. With technical and financial help from APEDA, UP has brought about marked changes in the quality and size of potatoes to match global standards. While exports in 2000-01 was limited to just about 100 tons, it had grown to 6,599.51 tons, valued at Rs. 317.54 million in 2004-05.

Fresh Fruits

In fresh fruits, the major items of export are mangoes, grapes, guava, papaya, pineapples and apples. Fresh mangoes went to more than 58 countries, valued at Rs. 1,707 million in 2008-09 up from Rs. 1,274.17 million in 2007-08. Major countries importing mangoes from India were UAE, Bangladesh, Nepal, and Saudi Arabia. Fresh grapes of the value of Rs. 4,086 to 49 countries, the major ones being Netherlands, UK, Bangladesh, Germany, Belgium and Nepal.

Fresh mangoes went to more than 58 countries, valued at Rs. 1,707 million in 2008-09 up from Rs. 1,274.17 million in 2007-08. The major markets for mangoes, of which India is the largest producer and exporter, are Bangladesh, UAE, Bahrain, Canada, France, Germany, UK, Hong Kong, Iran, Japan, Malaysia, Netherlands, Oman, Qatar, Russia, Saudi Arabia, Singapore, the USA and Yemen. Fresh mangoes worth Rs. 1,707.12 million were exported in 2008-09 as against Rs. 869.5 million in 2003-04 and Rs. 1,105.19 million in 2004-05.

Fresh grapes of the value of Rs. 4,086 to 49 countries, the major ones being Netherlands, the UK, Bangladesh, Germany, Belgium and Nepal. Other fresh fruits, valued at Rs. 3178.25 million went to 48 countries in 2007-08. Major countries, which imported fresh fruits from India were Bangladesh, Netherlands, the UK, UAE, Germany, Nepal and Germany.

Three new items in fresh fruits, introduced by Indian exporters — strawberries, pomegranates and lichis — are doing well. The export of the three items have more than doubled in four years from 2001-02.

Animal Products

Among animal products, the export of buffalo meat is the largest item of export, there being a ban on export of beef (meat of cow and its progeny). Buffalo meat fetched the country Rs. 48,397.10 million in 2008-09 as against Rs. 27,295.70 million in 2005-06. Compared to that, the export of sheep and goat meat was a poor Rs. 1,341 million in 2007-08 and Rs. 658.7 million in 2006-07. The exports of the item, however, skyrocketed to Rs. 4,933.69 million in 2008-09. With an export of Rs. 6,685.00 million, dairy products stood second in over all export of animal products. Next comes poultry products, which fetched the country Rs. 1,675.8 million.

India's exports of meat and meat preparations have registered a phenomenal growth in the last forty-five years. Malaysia has been the largest among 62 countries importing buffalo meat. Besides Malaysia, other major markets for buffalo meat were Philippines, Saudi Arabia, Angola, Jordan, UAE, Kuwait, Georgia, Oman, Korea Republic, Iran, Congo, Lithuania, Myanmar, Germany, Iraq, Vietnam, Armenia, Gabon, Hong Kong, Bahrain, Greece, Yemen, Qatar, Ivory Coast, Azerbaijan and Netherlands. Buffalo meat went to 36 other countries of lower values. Items in buffalo meat included meat of bovine animal with bone, boneless meat of bovine animal, carcasses of bovine animal (fresh), frozen carcasses of bovine animal, frozen meat of bovine animal with bone and frozen boneless meat of bovine animal.

Sheep and goat meat exports had a hefty growth of 176 per cent in 2003-04 over the previous year. However, in 2004-05, there was a decline of 28 per cent to Rs. 793.59 million. In 2005-06, there was a marginal rise to Rs. 803.7 million. Saudi

Arabia was India's biggest market for sheep and goat meat. UAE came next, followed by Qatar, Oman, Kuwait and Bahrain. Sheep and goat meat went to 17 other countries in smaller quantities.

Besides buffalo meat and meat of sheep and goat, ham and other meat of swine, and meat of fowls were exported in small quantities to fewer countries. India also exported animal casing with Jordon as a major importer. Other importers were Germany, Portugal, France, Kuwait, Spain and Turkey.

India also exported live fowls of species gallous domesticus, live ducks, geese, guinea fowls, live geese, turkeys and guinea fowls. APEDA, which promotes exports of agricultural products has sponsored delegations of meat exporters to Turkey, Iran and Jordan. APEDA also worked to expand exports of buffalo meat to Russia, Bulgaria, Saudi Arabia and Brazil. The Livestock and Meat Exporters Association (meat and meat products) is among private trade organization involved in the export of livestock and meat products.

It has been observed that in bulk of the export of animal products from India, value-addition was minimal. Thus, in meat of both bovine animal and sheep and goat, meat with bone, boneless meat, carcasses (fresh), frozen carcasses, frozen meat with bone and frozen boneless meat were exported. Processed meat too was exported, but of a much smaller value.

Further, animal products fall under the category of perishables. They need both refrigerated vans and cold storage facility at airports. Recently, the world's largest cold storage facility with a refrigerated area of 30,000 sq. ft., capable of handling up to 100,000 tons of perishable cargo per year was opened in Chatrapati Shivaji International Airport at Sahar in Mumbai. The facility was set up by APEDA and the Airport Authority of India. Similar facilities need to be opened at other airports in India to enable it to promote exports of perishables.

Marine Products

India has a vast coastline, where fishery is the main occupation of the people. Export of marine products far exceeded that of meat and meat preparations and dairy and poultry products taken together.

Export of marine products has set an all time record of US $1.48 billion (Rs. 66,466.9 million) during 2004-05. Exports further escalated to Rs. 86,079.4 million in 2008-09, steadily going up from Rs. 39.2 million in 1961-62, according to figures available from the Marine Products Export Development Authority.

Before 1960, markets for Indian marine products were largely confined to neighbouring countries like Sri Lanka, Myanmar, Singapore, etc. when our exports were dominated by dried items. This situation changed with the development of technology and modernization. Dried items gave way to canned and frozen items. With this, the more sophisticated and affluent markets like Japan, the USA, Europe and Australia became India's important buyers. Several seafood processing units with modern machinery for freezing and production of value-added products were set up at all important centers in the country for export processing.

For a long time, the USA was the principal buyer for our frozen shrimp but after 1977, Japan emerged as the principal buyer of the product, followed by the West European countries. Japan retained its position till 2001-02 as the single largest buyer for India's marine products accounting for about 31 per cent in the total export value. During the years 2002-03 and 2003-04 the USA emerged as the single largest market for our marine products. However, during the year 2004-05, the European Union has collectively become the largest importer of Indian marine products and it has retained its position since 2005-06.

During 2008-09, the European Union (EU) continued as the largest market with a percentage share of 32.6 in US dollar realization followed by China 14.8 per cent, Japan 14.6 per cent, USA 11.9 per cent, South East Asia 10%, Middle East 5.5% and other countries 10.6 per cent%.

However, largely due to the prevailing economic recession export to the EU, the USA and Japan declined 6.08 per cent, 10.18 per cent and 8.80 per cent respectively, while all other countries increased their import of marine products from India during the year.

Items like frozen Shrimp, Cuttlefish, Fish and Squid showed an increase in export, whereas dried items showed a declining trend. Export of Frozen Fin Fish also showed a positive growth both in share percentage as well as in growth percentage. Export of fish items, like ribbon fish, croaker, pomfret, tuna, seer fish, mackerel, grouper, fish fillets, fresh water fish, etc. showed increasing trend.

While the share of cuttlefish remained static, the export of frozen squid has registered substantial growth. The share of squid has also increased. Chilled items, frozen surmi, seafood mix, frozen crab stick, frozen crab, etc., also showed positive growth.

However, the export of dried items showed a drastic decline in growth as well as in share. This was mainly due to the decline in the export of dried jelly fish salted. Live items, like live crab, live aquarium fish, live snail showed a positive growth. The year 2004-05 saw export of new items such as fish burger, frozen crab cutlet, breaded squid ring and fish finger.

The USA re-emerged as the largest market for Indian marine products in 2005-06 after conceding the position to European Union in the previous year. The USA imported during the year marine products valued at over Rs.15,000 million, which amounted to more than 23 per cent of India's total marine exports during 2005-06.

Export to Japan has started showing a positive growth both in terms of quantity and value. Japan was the third largest importer of marine products from India during 2005-

06. Export to China, another major importer of marine products, declined by 11.93 per cent in 2005-06. Export to Australia too declined. The Middle East, South-east Asia, Canada, New Zealand, Turkey, Norway, Bulgaria showed a positive growth in 2004-05, whereas Switzerland, Poland, Lithuania, Guinea, Libya, Egypt, Bangladesh, etc. showed a declining trend.

Having a coastline of 8,129 km, India, according to FAO, has a fish production potential of 8.4 million tons a year. But presently, only around 6.5 million tons is being exploited. More than 90 per cent of fisheries output is being consumed domestically, and barely 25 per cent of marine fish caught is being exported.

Indian fishing sector is technologically underdeveloped and dominated by small fishermen, using traditional methods, catamarans and small fishing vessels. Most of the mechanized vessels are ill-equipped to undertake long voyages and lack specialized fishing equipment, such as fish finders, global positioning systems, refrigerated fish hold, refrigerated sea water systems and power. The lack of mother vessels, which can receive the harvest from smaller boats and chill or freeze the catch immediately and carry out some value addition on board is seen as another drawback.

The deep-sea sector has not been able to make a dent in the fishing sector, owing to technological gaps and lack of a progressive fishing policy designed to attract investment in the sector. Though the country has the largest number of processing units in the world approved to the EU standards, with a daily capacity of 10,250 tons of processed products, or about three million tons annually, only 24 per cent of the capacity is being presently utilized.

Although robust growth of exports of marine products was witnessed in the 80s and 90s when exports crossed US $1 billion level, the sector has witnessed stagnation in the last decade. Among the reasons attributed for this has been slow expansion of aquaculture owing to the shrimp disease problem and lack of diversification to export-oriented aquaculture.

Then of late, the Tsunami has adversely impacted India's marine products exports. The Tsunami had caused extensive damage to the fishing infrastructure, such as boats, nets and landing jetties, which is likely to affect the landing of fish and exports as well. The Government took necessary steps to build up infrastructure facilities afresh. The Government has also, through MPEDA, been implementing a number of schemes to boost the export of marine products. These schemes include extension of financial assistance to seafood processing industry, steps to upgrade processing facilities to meet international standards of hygiene and quality, expansion of aquaculture, imparting training to aquaculture farmers to adopt sound management practices to prevent outbreak of diseases and assistance to produce value added products for export and marketing.

Dairy and Poultry Products

Dairy and poultry industries have shown remarkable growth in India, which has now become one of the largest producers of milk and value-added milk products in the world. In the poultry sector, India is the fifth largest egg producer and 19th largest broiler producer. Also, India is one of the few countries to possess the technology for the production of pathogen free eggs. Exports of dairy and poultry products taken together have gone up more than ten-fold since 1995-96.

Besides milk, dairy products, including butter, processed cheese and cheese spread, milk powder and dairy whitener are produced in modern milk processing plants in the country. Milk and milk products are rated as one of the most promising sectors for India, which deserve foreign investment in a big way. When world milk production registered a negative growth of two per cent, India performed much better with 4 per cent growth. Total milk production in India is estimated to be around 72 million tons, while the demand is around 80 million tons. In the last six years, foreign investment in the sector stood at Rs. 3,600 million, which is about one-fourth of total investment made in the sector.

As in other perishable agricultural products, low value addition brought lower returns. Dairy products did include milk powders, condensed milk, fresh cheese, processed cheese, natural milk products, but mostly in low volume and value. Although exports of milk powders, in granules and other solid forms, have gone up over 25-fold between 2002-03 and 2004-05, exports of other milk products continued to be of low value. Exports of value-added products could be boosted if foreign collaboration is encouraged. Similarly, poultry products too need value addition and foreign collaboration, which could help exports.

India exported dairy products worth Rs. 3,891.38 million in 2004-05, which represented a hefty growth of 150.74 per cent over Rs. 1,551.9 million in the previous year. Exports of dairy products went up to a whopping Rs. 7,940.11 million in 2005-06 and further to Rs. 8665.63 million in 2007-08 and Rs. 9808.60 million in 2008-09. Exports of poultry products showed a decline of 31.34 per cent to Rs. 1,541 million during 2004-05 from Rs. 2,024 million in 2003-04. Exports poultry products, however, went up to 3,133.73 million in 2005-06 and further to Rs. 3181.70 million in 2006-07 and Rs. 4410.85 in 2007-08. Exports of poultry products, however, declined to Rs. 4,220.58 million in 2008-09.

Taken together, dairy and poultry products showed a growth of 51.91 per cent to Rs. 5,432.3 million in 2004-05 over Rs. 3,575 million in the previous year. Growth was nearly 100 per cent in 2005-06. This shows the potential for growth of the sector.

India's dairy products went to 71 countries during 2004-05. Bangladesh was India's largest market for dairy products. USA came next, followed by UAE, Germany, Algeria, Egypt and Nepal. Besides, India had sizeable markets for dairy products in Singapore, followed by Oman, Sri Lanka, Peoples Republic of China, Malaysia, Bhutan, Kuwait, Yemen Republic, Netherlands, Bahrain, Japan and Iran. Some of these markets expanded exponentially in 2004-05.

Nevertheless, India, known to be a country of milk, butter and cream, imported in 2005-06 milk and cream of the order of 1,633 tons valued at Rs.142.00 million. India imported milk and cream from 30 countries including Australia, Bahrain, Belgium, Bhutan, Canada, China, Ireland, Italy, Japan, Korea, Malaysia, Netherlands, New Zealand, Sri Lanka, Switzerland, Thailand, Turkey, UAE, the UK, the USA and Uruguay.

Poultry products exported included live poultry, eggs in shell, egg yolk dried, eggs not in shell (dried and cooled), eggs not in shell (frozen and preserved). India's poultry products went to 53 countries during 2004-05 with Japan, Oman, Germany, UAE, Kuwait, Saudi Arabia, Indonesia and China constituting major markets.

To boost dairy exports, the Indian Dairy Association has demanded for the dairy sector incentives provided to the agricultural sector under the "Vishesh Krishi Upaj Yojana" (Special Agricultural Production Plan) unveiled in the Trade Policy. Under the plan, exporters can freely import goods worth five per cent of the freight-on-board value of their exports and transfer this right if they do not want to use it. Besides, Agri-export Zones have been permitted duty-free import of capital goods and simpler import of restricted inputs.

Lack of infrastructure facilities, such as poultry disease diagnostic laboratories, feed analytical laboratories, meat testing laboratories, processing, packaging of broilers, including developing cold storage chains and cold storage transportation to and from airports and sea-ports and speedy handling of cargo, are major constraints, badly affecting Indian exports.

Lack of quality consciousness is another reason. Then comes brand building, which is not only expensive, but also time consuming. Besides, cost of export is also alarming compared to developed countries. The high incidence of customs and excise duties, absence of incentives for exports have been other major inhibiting factors.

The scope for boosting exports of both dairy and poultry products is tremendous if the constraints are attended to and steps taken to promote exports. Steps would also need to be taken to enhance domestic production, for with the increase in per capita income of the population, domestic consumption, which is far below what has been recommended by the National Committee on Human Nutrition, would go up, leaving a smaller surplus for exports, which would recede.

APEDA has also kept fruits and vegetable seeds and walnut among fresh fruits and vegetables. Walnuts worth Rs. 1620.78 and fruits and vegetable seeds worth Rs. 1421.23.

Floriculture

Floriculture is an upcoming trade with potential both in domestic and export markets. World over, flowers have gained an important place in one's life, be it for religious purposes or personal decoration. The global floriculture industry has been growing at an annual rate of 10 per cent to 12 per cent. The USA, Germany, the UK, Japan and the Netherlands are the major markets for flowers from India. Besides, Italy, Belgium, Poland, Australia are also coming up as large consuming countries.

Floriculture exports from India, according to APEDA figures, registered constant increase from 1993-94 onwards. Major flower categories exported from India included rhododendrons, roses, flowering plants (excluding roses and rhododendrons), fresh cut flowers and buds for bouquets and ornamental purposes, dried, dried and bleache cut flower and flower buds also for bouquets and ornamental purposes.

Floriculture exports from India have been growing at a compound annual growth rate (CAGR) of 15 per cent till recently. The exports went up from Rs. 601.4 million in 1996-97 to Rs. 2,994.1 million in 2005-06, showing constant rise, except in 2001-02. The growth has, however, been significantly affected by the recent global recession largely due to the *decline in demand in all the major markets. India's exports of floriculture products decreased by 41 per cent to US $84.5 million (Rs. 3,400 million) in 2007-08 from US $144 million (Rs. 6,530 million) in 2006-07, which further came down by 5.10 per cent in 2008-09. However, in rupee terms in 2008-09 exports of floriculture products from India increased marginally to Rs. 3,688.13.*

Flowers from India go to 102 countries in different parts of the world. The United States, India's biggest market, as also UK, Japan and Germany showed a decline in 2004-05 even though over the years these markets have grown several fold. The Netherlands was the only major market, which showed a growth. The growth has been attributed to the market facilitation Centre, set up by APEDA in Amsterdam.

Italy, Belgium, UAE and Australia were some of the other emerging markets. China witnessed an upsurge in 2004-05, with 508 per cent growth in exports over the previous year. This is significant since China is herself an exporter of flowers.

Cut flowers used in bouquets, both fresh and dried were the most popular items from India. The USA again was the largest market for cut flowers for bouquets. Japan came next, followed by the UK, Germany, the Netherlands, Italy, Australia, Belgium, Switzerland and Singapore. The major flowers in the category – cut flowers for bouquets – are rose, gladiolus, tuberose, carnation, orchids, lillium, gerbera, chrysanthemum and gypsophila. The demand for Indian roses, appears to be going down. Only 13 countries imported roses from India in 2004-05.

Japan emerged as the largest market for Indian roses, followed by Mexico, Netherlands, Israel, UAE, Lebanon and UK. United States, which bought Rs. 691,841 worth of roses from India in 2003-04 did not buy at all in 2004-05. Singapore, Saudi Arabia, Sri Lanka, Kuwait, France, Chinese Taipei and Australia, which had been buying roses from India in earlier years, also failed to buy at all in 2003-04. In 2001-02, Kuwait was India's largest market for roses, with chiports worth Rs. 6.29 million worth.

The government has sanctioned more than 192 export-oriented units (EOUs) for floriculture. However, not more than one-third of them have become operational, says a report. Further, as mentioned earlier APEDA, as part of its continued efforts to support the floriculture industry and promote floriculture export, had set up a 'Marketing Facilitation Centre' in Amsterdam (The Netherlands). The Centre became operational in November 2001. According to APEDA, the Centre helped secure increase in volume and unit value realization of floriculture products, reduction in rejections, improved customer feedback, direct market contacts and in confidence building. It also assisted the exporters in negotiations for final rates and prices.

State governments too have been helping in giving a boost to the floriculture industry. Lately, the Maharashtra Industrial Development Corporation (MIDC) has set apart 150 acres of land and an investment of Rs. 2,000 million for a floriculture park.

Meanwhile, the TATA Economic Consultancy Services, Mumbai, which had been appointed as Consultant for examining the rehabilitation package, submitted by floriculture units to their respective banks, has in its report submitted that 28 units could be revived.

The reason for the units not taking off so far was that floriculture was a low-priced product, whilst the infrastructure costs were high. It was not only necessary to reduce the bush cost, but also the infrastructure cost, which should be brought down to Rs. 5 million from the present Rs. 12.5 million to Rs. 15 million per hectare. Floriculture units, the report said, should be brought under the EOF (Export Oriented Farms) so that it could come under the Ministry of Agriculture.

The geographic location of the country, which is quite central in terms of logistics, being in the centre of two growing markets—Europe and South-east Asia—should help it in promoting its exports of the item. Proximity to the growing market in the Gulf region too is an advantage. According to an ASSOCHAM study, lack of proper infrastructure, plant material, production technology, non-availability of basic inputs and cold storage facilities to handle such exports efficiently have all acted as bottlenecks to this sector. To boost floriculture exports, India should go in for potential export items like cut flowers, dry flowers, seeds, potted plants and micro-propagated plantlets.

Further, as suggested by the TATA Economic Consultancy Services, the existing export-oriented units for floriculture should be converted into EOF so that they could get the incentives available with the Ministry of Agriculture. Further, the corporate sector should be encouraged to take part in floriculture as in other areas of agriculture through contract farming. The Agriculture Ministry, the state governments, the corporate sector and APEDA should all work together to exploit the full potential of floriculture for exports.

6

Agricultural and Allied Products—Non-perishable

Processed fruits and vegetables, dried and preserved fruits and vegetables, cereals and pulses, rice, wheat, spieces, beverages, sugar, cashew and ground nut, vegetable oil fixed edible and castor oil.

Besides perishable food items, India's exports, as also its imports, consist of non-perishable food items. The items include processed fruits and vegetables, food grains and pulses, beverages, and sugar and molasses.

India's imports of non-perishable food items include wheat, rice, other cereals, cereals preparations, pulses, tea, cashew nut, nuts other than cashew nuts, spices, sugar, oilseeds, vegetable oils (fixed edible), some of them of much lower value. In 2005-06, it did not import wheat at all, whereas it imported pulses of more than twice the value of its exports of the item. On the other hand, India imported vegetable oils (fixed edible) of a high value and did not export the item at all. It also imported sugar of a higher value compared to its exports. Its imports of spices was, however, one third of its exports of the item.

Processed Foods

India grows a variety of temperate to tropical fruits and vegetables. Processing plays an important role in the conservation and effective utilization of fruits and vegetables. It also helps in generating rural employment.

Of late, food processing, particularly of fruits and vegetables, is emerging as a major growth center in Indian *industry, what with Reliance, Pantaloon, Godrej, Field Fresh, Bharti Enterprises joint venture with Rothschild, Ballarpur industries, Tata Group and Mahindra and Mahindra drawing up big plans in the agro-foods segment. Reliance alone is said to have plans to invest over Rs. 40,000 million, mostly in Punjab and Haryana into agri-business. The market for India's processed food is officially assessed at US $30 billion.*

India is the world's second largest producer of fruits and vegetables after the United States, accounting for 10 per cent of global share. Out of 370 million tons of fruit production in the world, India accounts for 30 million tons. Of the 456 million tons of vegetable produced in the world, India's share is 59 million tons, amounting to 17 per cent.

India has favourable climatic conditions and vast potential for growing fruits and vegetables. However, less than 1.5 per cent of the total production of fruits and vegetables is processed at present in units covered under the Food Production Order. Preserved vegetables exported by India include dried potatoes, dried mushrooms, preserved onions, dehydrated onion flakes, dehydrated garlic powder, preserved cucumber and gherkins, spinach frozen, frozen peas and potatoes, peas dried and shelled, mixed vegetables frozen and assorted canned vegetables. the UAE, the UK, Bangladesh, Saudi Arabia, Germany, France, Netherlands, the USA, Sri Lanka, Indonesia and Philippines are India's major markets for preserved fruits and vegetables.

Major items in processed fruits and vegetables include mango pulp and pickles and chutneys. Mango pulp went to over 69 countries, of the total value of Rs. 3,642.40 million in 2005-06, which went up to Rs. 5096.85 million in 2007-08 and further to Rs. 7529.89 million in 2008-09. Saudi Arabia with imports worth Rs. 1,023.76 million was India's principal market during the year. It was followed by Yemen Arab Republic, UAE, Kuwait, the UK, Japan, the USA, Sudan, France, Germany, Lebanon, Netherlands, Canada, Russia, Malaysia, Finland, Bahrain, Bangladesh and Jordon.

India exported pickles and chutnies to over seventy countries, which included Russia, the USA, Belgium, Netherlands, Spain, Estonia, France, Canada, Ukraine and Germany. India's exports of pickles and chutneys were of the order of Rs. 5,096.85 million in 2007-08, going up from Rs. 2,609.81 million in 2005-06. Growth in 2005-06 was 100 per cent compared to Rs. 1,293.5 million in the previous year. Pickles exported included those of chilly, green pickles, mango pickles, while chutneys included those of mango, tomato, lemon and tamarind concentrate.

India's exports of processed and preserved fruits and vegetables have grown by 320 per cent to Rs. 14,627.2 million in 2004-05 from Rs. 3,480 million in 1994-95 and further to Rs. 18,682.03 million in 2008-09. Processed fruits exported by India included mango steens (sliced and dried), mango pulp, mango slices in brine, dried apricots and apples. Jams and jellies of apple, guava, mango and pineapple have their own markets. Then there are the juices of grape fruit, lemon, mango squash, orange juice and frozen orange squash. Major markets for mangosteen are Bangladesh, the UK and Saudi Arabia.

Major items in the export of processed fruits and vegetables include mango pulp and pickles and chutneys. India is one of the leading mango pulp producing countries. Mango pulp went to over 69 countries, of the total value of Rs. 3,642.40 million in 2005-06,which went up to Rs. 5096.85 million in 2007-08 and further to Rs. 7,529.89 million in 2008-09. Saudi Arabia with imports worth Rs. 1,023.76 million was India's principal market during the year. It was followed by Yemen Arab Republic, UAE, Kuwait, the UK, Japan, the USA, Sudan, France, Germany, Lebanon, Netherlands, Canada, Russia, Malaysia, Finland, Bahrain, Bangladesh and Jordon.

Pickles and chutneys worth Rs. 2,506.17 million were exported to 55 countries in 2007-08, according to APEDA. This represented a decline from Rs. 2,935.94 million in 2006-07. This was second successive year of decline with exports worth Rs. 2,609.81 million in 2005-06. Exports in 2004-05 and

2003-04 were of the order of Rs. 1,293.46 million and Rs. 1,197.47 million respectively.

Chilly pickles worth Rs. 52 million were exported to 29 countries, including USA, UK, Canada, Australia, Malaysia, Saudi Arabia and UAE in 2002-03. Green pickles worth Rs. 16.9 million were exported to 16 countries and mango pickles worth Rs. 107.19 million to 33 countries. Mango chutney, tomato chutney, tamarind concentrate chutney were also exported, although to lesser number of countries and in smaller quantities.

A number of large national and multi-national companies have now entered the processed food industries with a thrust on exports. Products like vegetable curries, dals (pulses), sweets, etc in improved packaging have been introduced for reaching the new markets. The growth in this group is contributed by pulses, processed fruits and juices and processed vegetables.

Squashes and Juices

India's exports of squashes and juices have received a big thrust, with exports of the two items going up to Rs. 750 million in 2007-08, compared to around Rs. 475 million in 2005-06. Squashes exported included those of mango, lemon, pineapple, grapes, apple, guava, fruit cocktail and others. Juices were those of orange, grapes, pineapple and others.

Besides fruits and vegetables, other processed and preserved foods include crisp bread, ginger bread, wafers, rusks, roasted bread and similar roasted products, pastries, cakes, biscuits and other bakers wares, papads, chocolate and confectionary, chocolate and other food preparations containing cocoa, malted milk, chewing gum and other sugar confectionery, cocoa butter and paste. These items went to a large number of countries including the UK, the USA, Canada, Germany, France, UAE, Qatar, Singapore, Malaysia, Hong

Kong, Korea, Philippines, South Africa, besides neighbouring countries, like Nepal, Bangladesh and Sri Lanka.

To promote exports, India would do well to have collaboration with multi-nationals to process fruits and vegetables. The exports of the two items in value-added form would yield much higher returns than what is available from fresh fruits and vegetables. What people in developed countries need is ready to eat packed food items rather than fresh fruits and vegetables. India should, therefore, promote the production of packed food items to have a much larger share of the global market in fruits and vegetable.

India imported cereal preparations worth Rs. 300.94 million from over 65 countries in 2005-06. Detailed figures of imports of cereal preparations is not available. While Agricultural and Processed Food Products Export Development Authority (APEDA) provides export statistics for agro and food products, there is no similar institution to provide details of imports.

Cereals and Pulses

India has long surpassed the stage, when it was dependent on imports of food grains for meeting the needs of its population. From the stage when it was import-dependent, India has in the nineties reached a stage when it is exporting all major food grains – pulses, rice basmati, rice other than basmati, wheat and other grains — the world over. Exports of food grains and pulses have gone up from Rs. 50,836.17 million in 1995-96 to Rs. 72,326.20 million in 2005-06. The production and exports of food grains and pulses are, however, heavily dependent on rains.

Pulses

Pulses from India worth Rs. 5,490 million went to over 80 countries in 2007-08. Pakistan was the largest market, importing Rs. 1,419.88 million worth in 2007-08. Other major markets were the USA, the UK, Nepal, UAE, Malaysia, Sri Lanka, Saudi Arabia and Kuwait. The exports of the item, however, registered sharp decline from 451,626 tons, valued at Rs. 11,246 million in 2005-06 to 255,084 tons valued at Rs. 7,899 million in 2006-07 and further to 170,614 tons valued at Rs 5,490 million in 2007-08. India has been exporting masoor, gram, moong, tur, urd and other pulses.

Sharp fall in imports by the USA, the UK, Bangladesh Saudi Arabia, Malaysia, and Mauritius among others in 2007-08 led to the decline in exports of pulses by India. Imports by the USA fell from Rs. 640.28 million in 2006-07 to Rs. 56.27 million in 2007-08, by Bangladesh from Rs. 1,814 million to nil, by the UK from Rs. 298.4 million to Rs. 37.03 million, by Saudi Arabia from Rs. 437.48 million to Rs. 209.67 million, by Nepal from Rs. 259.58 million to Rs. 6.65 million, by Malaysia from 72.47 million to Rs. 43.22 million and by Mauritius from Rs. 38.29 million to Rs. 1.86 million.

Rice

Among food grains, basmati rice, which means the "queen of fragrance" has been the favoured one. The export of basmati rice has gone up from 597,793 tons worth Rs. 18,769.00 million in 1998-99 to 1.16 million tons, valued at Rs. 30,430.92 million in 2005-06. Exports of basmati rice went up further to Rs. 43,445.80 million in 2007-08. Basmati rice has been grown in foothills of Himalayas for thousands of years. Its perfumery, nut-like flavour and aroma makes it the costliest rice in the world and has been the choice of emperors and praised by poets for hundreds of years. There are three types of basmati rice-golden parboiled, raw basmati and silky raw basmati.

India has been famous for its basmati rice, so much so that the United States granted a patent in 1997 to its company, Rice Tec Inc, for a similar strain developed by it, calling it "Kasmati", or "Texmati". Taking advantage of the patent, the American company has been trying to enter the international market, but with minimal success.

The export of rice other than basmati registered a steep decline in 2003-04 to 2.64 million tons from 4.25 million tons in the previous year. In 2004-05, exports again went up to 3.61 million tons. It was, nevertheless, nowhere near the peak of 4.36 million tons valued at Rs. 44,036.45 million in 1998-99. Non-basmati rice is the staple diet of a large proportion of the country's population and perhaps this is the reason for the decline in its exports. With drought-like conditions in 2003-04, the country could neither have the surplus, nor the inclination to export in large quantities.

On the other hand, India imported rice to the tune of Rs. 260 tons valued at Rs. 3.43 million from Italy, Republic of Korea, Saudi Arabia, USA and Vietnam.

Wheat

Exports of wheat reached its peak in 2003-04, going up to 4.02 million tons, valued at Rs. 2,349.36 million from 3.67 million tons valued at Rs. 1,759.86 million in the previous year, despite forecasts to the contrary in certain circles. Exports in 2005-06 were of the order of 746,173.23 tons, valued at Rs. 5,575.2 million and in 2006-07 46,633.21 tons, valued at Rs. 353.09 million. In 2007-08, exports fell sharply to 237.27 tons, valued at Rs. 2.39 million. India produces both durum and aestivum varieties of wheat, but is a major durum wheat producer. Exporters have reportedly been facing acute shortage of rail wagons recently to move wheat from government warehouses in Punjab and Haryana to export ports, resulting in high demurrage costs.

This problem, according to reports, is likely to persist in view of government's priority to move grains to deficient areas and for drought relief operations. India did not import wheat in 2005-06. However, in 2006-07 it is estimated to have imported 1.47 million tons of wheat of the value of Rs. 1,473.35 million.

Exports of other cereals, which include rye, maize, bajra, jowar, ragi and sorghum, were of the order of 570,301 tons in 2003-04, compared to 106,076 tons in 2002-03. The exports of other cereals again went up to 1,178,029 tons in 2004-05, but went down to 653,688 tons in 2005-06. Exports of other cereals have gone up to 3,228,051.70 tons valued at Rs. 30,023.29 million in 2007-08 from 28,097 tons in 1995-96, recording a growth of 4,207 per cent. India's major export destinations for other cereals in 2007-8 were Malaysia, Saudi Arabia, Republic of Korea, Taiwan and UAE.

India imported other cereals to the tune of 27,884 tons of the value of Rs. 300.94 million in 2005-06 from 14 countries, including UK and USA. India also imported 1.69 million tons of pulses valued at Rs. 2,476.24 million from over 42 countries in 2005-06.

Bangladesh has been a major market for India's food grains and pulses, importing in large quantities. Other major markets included Sri Lanka, UAE, the UK, Ukraine, Nepal, Saudi Arabia, the USA, Malaysia and Yemen. Basmati rice has been going to 81 countries, rice other than basmati to 116 countries, wheat to 53 countries, other cereals to 89 countries and pulses to 102 countries. Besides the above-mentioned countries, rice other than basmati has been going to Cameroon, Djibouti, Gabon, Maldives and Kuwait. Wheat has also been going to Philippines, Sudan, Vietnam and Yemen.

Weather improving in coming years leading to larger production, there is vast scope for exports of food grains and pulses. As is evident from figures available from DGCI&S, exports of rice basmati has not been affected much by the patent granted to the American company, Rice Tec Inc., except of course to United States itself. However, opposition has been voiced within the country whether it should undertake export of food grains, particularly on a scale as is being done at present, when the people of the country have not been getting per capita nutrients as prescribed by specialists. To meet this situation, all out effort should be made to increase production.

Spices

India is a leading producer and exporter of spices in the world. In recent years, export of Indian spices has taken giant leaps. From traditional commodity exports, Indian spices have evolved into a state-of-the-art industry, absorbing technology, broad-basing its products range, developing value-added products, identifying niche markets, forging strategic alliances and clinching global collaborations and joint ventures. India produces 2.5 to 3.0 million tons of spices annually. The country produces spices of different categories worth about US $3 billion. Out of 109 spices listed by ISO, 63 are grown in India. The country accounts for 25-30 per cent of world's pepper production, 35 per cent of ginger and about 90 per cent of turmeric.

However, India also imported 108,925 tons of spices valued at Rs. 6,878.11 million in 2005-06 from 94 countries.

India produces and exports a large variety of spices—pepper, cardamom, small and large, turmeric, coriander, cumin, celery, fennel, fenugreek, garlic, nutmeg and mace, vanilla, curry powder mixture, mint products, spice oils and oleoresins. Besides, it produces and exports seed spices, including mustard, aniseed, bishop's weed (ajwain seed), dill seed, poppy seed, etc. It also exports other miscellaneous spices, including tamarind, asafetida, cambodge, cassia, saffron spices, etc. Mint products exported by it include mint oils, menthol and menthol crystal.

No country in the world produces as many kinds of spices as India. Currently, India produces around 2.5 million tons of different spices, valued approximately at US $3 billion and holds the premier position in the world. Almost all spices are grown in the country because of its varying climates, from tropical to sub-tropical. In almost all the 25 States and seven Union Territories in the country, at least one spice is grown in abundance.

India commands a formidable position in the world spices market, with a 37 per cent share in volume and 27 per cent in *value in 2003-04. Indian spices go to more than 157 countries in all the continents. India exported 615,000 tons of spices valued at Rs. 43,115 million in 2007-08, more than double that of 244,9000 tons, valued at Rs. 16,190 million in 2000-2001. Exports in 2005-06 were of the order of 350,303 tons valued at Rs. 26,276.2 million. The largest exports in terms of value has been that of mint products, i.e., Rs. 5,021.9 million (US $ 111.99 million). However, the most popular item, going to almost all countries to which spices are exported by India, is pepper – 14,148 metric tons, valued at Rs. 1,217.1 million (US $27.14 million) in 2004-05.*

Spice oil and oleoresins constituted items of bulk exports, valued at Rs. 4,693.1 million (US $ 104.64 million) in 2004-05,. Chili was also a major item with exports of 138,073 MT, valued at Rs. 4,990.3 million (US $111.28 million). Exports of turmeric in 2004-05 was 43,097 tons valued at Rs. 1,562.5 million.

As in the case of many other commodities, United States happened to be the largest market for Indian spices importing 42,402 metric tons in 2004-05, worth Rs. 5,000.03 million, according to Spices Board. Malaysia with imports of Rs. 1,484.97 million, proved to be the country's second largest market in 2004-05. The UK emerged third with imports of 15,391 mt valued at Rs. 1,345.9 million. Germany, China, Japan, Bangladesh, Sri Lanka, UAE, Singapore, France, Saudi Arabia, Spain, the Netherlands and Indonesia were other major markets.

Some of the distant Latin American countries too were emerging as markets for Indian spices. Latin American countries importing Indian spices included Brazil, Argentina, Chile, Costa Rica, Mexico, Paraguay, Peru, Uruguay and Venezuela.

The consumers of spices the world over are becoming more and more quality conscious. The importing countries are stipulating more stringent quality requirements year after year. The Spices Board has launched various programmes for educating farmers, traders and exporters in improving the quality of Indian spices to meet requirements of the consumers globally. In recent years, organic agriculture has been gaining considerable importance. The demand for organically produced foods is growing rapidly in developed countries of Europe, as also in the USA, Japan and Australia.

Many farmers today show interest in organic cultivation and several of them have begun switching to this traditional method of cultivation as a means to produce safe food stuffs and preserve environment. Already, the country is exporting organic spices of around 50 tons of different varieties. The quantity is, however, too small considering that we are exporting around 250,000 tons of spices annually.

The Spices Board, as part of its export promotion programme, is providing financial assistance to exporters registered with it for printing promotional brochures and folders on spices and spice products for distribution to overseas markets, for sending samples abroad, for participating in fairs abroad and for innovative packaging of spice products.

The assistance is 50 per cent of expenditure with a ceiling of Rs. 200,000 in the case of promotional brochures and folders and a maximum of Rs. 50,000 for sending samples of spices to buyers abroad. For renting out stalls, as also for innovative packaging, the ceiling is Rs. 200,000.

The Spices Board together with Indian Spices Export Forum has been organizing bi-annually the World Spices Congress, which has been another vehicle for the promotion of spices export. Attracting participants from more than 40 countries across the globe, the Congress also has a well-designed exhibition, which showcases the spice products on offer and the level of processing technology.

With more and more farmers taking to organic farming and with the assistance being provided by the Spices Board, it is hoped that the export of spices would grow manifold both in quantity and value terms in the coming years. What is noticeable is that India was also a major importer of spices.

India imported in 2005-06 spices of the order of 108,926,569 kg, valued at Rs. 6,878.12 million. Spices came to India from 94 countries.

Beverages

India exports to developing and developed countries not only fruits and vegetables and their preparations, but also alcoholic and non-alcoholic beverages. India has been exporting Indian-made foreign liquor to neighbouring South Asian, South-east Asian and West Asian countries, as also to Europe and the United States. Alcoholic beverages worth Rs. 3385.62 million was exported in 2007-08 as against Rs. 1,137.81 million in 2004-05, with European countries, including the United Kingdom, Germany, the Netherlands, besides Canada and the USA, importing them in significant quantities. Exports of spirit and beverages went up to Rs. 2,09.16.4 million in 2005-06.

Non-alcoholic beverages, like squashes, fruit juices, lemonade and mineral and aerated waters were also exported to Europe to quench the thirst of people in some of these countries of cold climes, which have over the past several years been experiencing extreme heat in summer months.

Export of alcoholic beverages by India have shown constant rise from 2002-03 onwards when they stood at Rs. 200.20 million. India's exports of alcoholic beverages include beer made from malt, wine, brandy, liquors, whiskies, Scotch, blended whiskies, rum and gin, according to provisional figures available from Agricultural Products Export Development Authority (APEDA).

United Kingdom, the mother of alcoholic beverages, imported from India during 2007-08, Rs. 11.40 million worth of the beverages, including beer made from malt. The USA imported beer. The Netherlands and Turkey imported during the year Bourbon Whisky. Canada imported beer and other alcoholic beverages. Other developed countries importing alcoholic beverages from India were Singapore, Hong Kong, Japan, and Australia.

In West Asia, UAE, Angola, Oman, Qatar, Bahrain were other major markets for India. In South-east Asia, besides Singapore, other countries importing alcoholic beverages were Thailand, Vietnam, Malaysia. Among neighbouring countries, Bhutan and Nepal were among major buyers.

About squashes and fruit juices, the Neitherlands, UK, Nepal and Russia were major markets for mango squash in 2007-08. The UK was again the largest buyer of lemon squash. Oman was the largest market for orange squash, while Russia, Nepal and Poland were major buyers for pineapple squash.

Japan was the largest among three importers of fruit cocktail squash followed by Czech Republic. Nepal was foremost among three buyers of grape squash. Italy, Nepal and UK were the only three buyers for apple squash. Other non-alcoholic beverages exported by India included orange juice, grape juice, apple juice, mango juice and mixture of juices.

India exported during 2007-08 mineral water worth Rs. 8.75 million and lemonade worth Rs. 5.19 million. Mineral water went to United Kingdom, Nepal and the United States among other countries, while lemonade went among others to the USA, Nepal, UAE and Maldives. India also exported ice cream and other edible ice to Singapore, Fiji and South Africa.

Exports of alcoholic beverages, squashes and fruit juices, aerated and mineral water should have good scope, considering that a number of industrialized and developed countries were importing them. Exports from India have gone up with the entry of PepsiCo with Florida-based Tropicana brand orange juice. Inevitably, growth in exports were limited considering the local demand, which necessitates higher production levels. This question is being tackled with the setting up of Agri-export Zones.

Sugar

India is a dominant player in the global sugar industry along with Brazil in terms of production. Production, however, is of a cyclical nature. Two to three years of high production is followed by two to three years of low production. Sugar production fell from 26.3 million tons in 2007-08 sugar season to 14.6 million tons in 2008-09 sugar season, according to provisional estimates carried by the Economic Survey 2009-2010. Sugar production went up to 19 million tons in 2005-06 season as against 13.5 million tons in the 2004-05 season.

The process of making sugar by evaporating juice from sugarcane was developed in India around 500 BC. Sugarcane, a tropical grass, is stated to have originated in New Guinea. During pre-historic times, its culture spread throughout the Pacific Islands and into India.

Production of sugar by India in 2003-04 has been estimated at 14.5 million tons which was 27.97 per cent lower than the all time high production of 20.13 million tons in the previous year. India's exports of sugar too went down from 1.66 million tons valued at Rs. 17,694.91 million in 2002-03 to 1.18 million tons, valued at Rs. 12,014.28 million in 2003-04. Exports in 2005-06 were 321,205 tons valued at Rs. 5,691.05 million.

Besides, India also imported 558,769 tons of sugar valued at Rs. 6,515.07 million in 2005-06, showing that imports were more than exports during the year. In addition, India's exports of molasses, a by-product in the production of sugar, amounted to Rs. 191.16 million in 2003-04, as against Rs. 540.46 million in the previous year. India's exports of sugar and molasses, taken together went down further to 116,848 tons valued at Rs. 1,550.52 million in 2004-05. In a happy augury, however, the exports of sugar and molasses shot up to 394,144 tons, valued at Rs. 5,979.10 million in 2005-06, according to figures available from DGCI&S.

India'a sugar industry is highly fragmented with organized and unorganized players. The unorganized players mainly produce Gur and Khandsari, the less refined forms of sugar. There were 507 sugar factories in the country as on May 31, 2004 with installed capacity of 17.87 million tons. Of these, 174 were in the private sector, 33 in the public or the state sector, while 300 were in the cooperative sector. The major sugar producing States are Andhra Pradesh, Bihar, Gujarat, Haryana, Karnataka, Madhya Pradesh, Maharashtra, Orissa, Tamil Nadu and Uttar Pradesh.

The production and sale, including export of sugar have been highly regulated till recently. Sugar and sugarcane, from which sugar is produced, have been Essential Commodities under the Essential Commodities Act, 1955. The Government has been following a policy of partial control and dual pricing of sugar. Under this policy, a certain percentage of sugar, produced by sugar factories was requisitioned by Government as compulsory levy at prices fixed by it in every sugar season. The levy sugar is distributed through the Public Distribution System (PDS), while free sale sugar is allowed to be sold as per the quantity released by the Government.

India has emerged as the largest producer of sugar in the world today. The Budget for the financial year 2002-03 announced complete decontrol of sugar, which led to a panic situation among sugar mill owners and a huge quantity of sugar was offloaded in the open market resulting in lowering of sugar prices affecting their financial position. In view of this, the Government postponed the decontrol of sugar industry by two years, i.e. till September 2005.

As regards exports, it was being carried out through notified export agencies like the State Trading Corporation (STC) and Indian Sugar and General Industry Export Import Corporation (ISGIEIC). On January 1, 1997, the Sugar Export Promotion Act, 1958 was repealed and sugar export was de-canalized with quantitative restrictions fixed by the government and registration-cum-allocation certificates issued by APEDA. On April 1, 2001, the government lifted the quantitative ceiling and registration requirement. The government lifted the ban on the export of sugar in January 2007.

India exports sugar to more than 95 countries. Sri Lanka with imports valued at Rs. 82.08 million happened to be

India's largest market in 2004-05, followed by Belgium, Maldives and Bangladesh.

The year 2005-06 is a watershed year with Pakistan importing Rs. 1,303.60 million worth of sugar from India as against Rs. 23.71 million worth in the previous year. Imports by Sri Lanka, Indonesia, Portugal and the USA too showed significant thrust.

India exports molasses to less than a score of countries. Major markets in 2005-06 were Nepal and Italy. Besides sugar and molasses, India exported cane jaggery (raw sugar) and palmyra jaggery to nearly 50 countries. The biggest market for cane jaggery was Portugal with imports worth Rs. 457.20 million in 2005-06, followed by Malaysia, Nepal, UAE, the USA, Bhutan, UK, Canada and Saudi Arabia. Palmyra jaggery was imported by Saudi Arabia, Sri Lanka, Romania, Syria, Iran, Canada, Malaysia, the USA and UAE.

The Indian urban market is slowly moving towards branded sugar. With the increase in production of sugar, more importantly of branded sugar, the potential for exports should also go up. However, with India's principal markets for sugar–Bangladesh, Indonesia, Malaysia, Sri Lanka and countries in West Asia-setting up their own refineries, exports of white sugar is likely to go down in the coming years and the country may have to export raw sugar.

Cashew and Groundnut

India also traded in cashew nut and ground nut. India exported 137,000 tons of cashew kernels valued at Rs. 29,311 million in 2008-09 Exports of ground nut were of the order of Rs. 10,540 million in value in 2007-08 as against Rs. 7,984.6 million in the previous year.

Besides ground nut, India exported a number of oil-bearing seeds such as sesame seed, niger seeds, other fruit and vegetable seeds and oil meals. India exported in 2008-09 sesame seeds worth Rs. 14,942 million, Guergam meal worth

Rs. 13,389.85 million, oil meals worth Rs. 102,692 million, niger seeds worth Rs. 642.98 million and fruits and vegetable seeds worth Rs. 11,199.80 million.

Vegetable Oil (Fixed Edible)

India imported 6.71 million tons of vegetable oil (edible) worth Rs. 158,190 million in 2008-09. India has been importing vegetable oil from more than 34 countries, including Indonesia, Argentina, Malaysia, Brazil, UAE and the United States.

Castor Oil

While India has been importing edible oil, it has exported castor oil. The exports in 2008-09 were of the order of Rs. 21,287.18 million. The exports have been mainly to the United States, China, France and Japan.

7
Plantation

(Tea, coffee and rubber, cashew nut and pepper, which too figure under plantation crops, are being dealt with under agriculture and allied products-non-perishable).

India has been rated as the world's largest producer and consumer of tea, producing some of the world's finest teas, as also the largest variety. India is also the seventh largest producer of coffee, described as "wonderful stimulant." Rubber is another plantation crop, one in which the exports of value added product is very high. (Cashew nut and pepper too figure under plantation, but have been dealt with under agriculture and allied products—non-perishable).

Tea

India's 13,000-odd tea gardens with a workforce of more than two million have made Indian tea the pride of the world in stores synonymous with luxury, such as Harrods. Among the famous specialty flavours of tea are Darjeeling tea and Assam tea from the north east and Nilgiri tea from the south.

India's tea production during 2007 was 986.43 million kg, as against 981.80 million kg in 2006. In 2008, tea production declined to 980.83 million kg, but was higher than 892 million kg in 2004, according to figures available with the Tea Board.

Export of tea from India during 2008-09 went up to 190.63 million kg, valued at Rs. 23,817.93 million, as against 185.32 million kg, valued at Rs. 185.32 million in the previous year. Tea export in 2005-06 was 162.85 million kg valued at

Rs. 17,307.27 million, down from 183.40 million kg., valued at Rs. 18,402.98 million, in 2004-05. Exports in 2003-04 were of the order of 177.80 million kg, valued at Rs.16,370 million, according to the data available with the Directorate General of Commercial Intelligence and Statistics (DGCI&S).

In spite of being the world's largest producer and exporter of tea, India imported 18.71 million kg of tea of the value of Rs. 1,081.4 million, among others, from Nepal, Vietnam and Kenya in 2005-06. Nepal exported to India the maximum quantity of 4.62 million kg.

Having a long time look, tea exports have gone down in quantitative terms to 190.64 million kg in 2008-09 from 199 million kg. in 1960-61. In terms of value, however, tea exports have gone up from Rs. 1,240 million in 1960-61 to Rs. 23,817.93 million in 2008-09. In 1980-81, exports of tea were a high of 229 million kg, although in terms of value the realisation was only Rs. 4,260 million (US $538 million).

Lately, India's tea exports to its largest market, the Russian Federation, has slumped following the break-up of the Federation in nineties. Russia is reported to be sourcing teas from China, as it is cheaper due to lower transportation costs. Some good quality Orthodox teas from Vietnam are also going to Russia. In addition, exporters from Sri Lanka, Kenya and new tea-producing countries, like Indonesia and Vietnam, are aggressively going after India's markets as the country's tea exporters remain complacent.

Further, in the domestic market multinational beverage companies like Coca Cola and Pepsi are drawing away Indian tea-drinkers. Things aren't good on the global front either, where the demand for Indian tea has been declining at an average rate of 1.5 per cent a year. In the high-value markets like the United States, Japan, the United Kingdom and the rest of Europe, India's competitors, Sri Lanka and Kenya, rule the roost. However, the situation has changed with Pakistan and West Asia emerging as major markets. Improved political relations with Pakistan and an MoU signed between Indian Tea Association (ITA) and Pakistan Tea Association

(PTA) in August 2003 helped exports to that country. In 2004-05, Iraq emerged as the second major market for Indian tea after the Russian Federation, importing 28.69 million kg. while UAE took the third position after the Russian Federation and Iraq, importing 24.28 million kg. The Russian Federation imported 36.87 million kg in 2004-05, which had a value realization of Rs. 2,724.5 million. It is worth taking note that despite the break-up of the Soviet Union, the Russian Federation continued to be the largest market for Indian tea, although in the very next year, i.e. in 2005-06, there was a decline to 33.10 million kg, valued at Rs. 2,410.9 million, although the Russian Federation continued to be on top. In calendar 2008, Russia imported from India 40 million kg of tea.

The global recession has not had any impact on India's tea exports, according to Mr. Basudeb Bannerji, Chairman of the Tea Board. For calendar 2008, tea exports from India stood at 196 million kg., up 10 per cent over 178 million kg. exported in 2007. Buoyed by the success of its efforts in West Asia, the tea board is now eyeing newer markets in Latin America. They are looking at market, such as Chile. Further, it is looking at China as a market for the country's black tea, according to reports in the Indian media.

Of the total Indian tea market, branded packaged teas account for 33-35 per cent by volume. Hindustan Lever (HLL) leads with around 43-45 per cent market share of the packaged tea, while Tata Tea comes next with around 17-18 per cent market share. Apart from these two players and Duncans, the market is extremely fragmented with many smaller regional players.

The other major items in tea trade are tea bags and instant tea. In 2008-09, India exported 10.25 million kgs of packet tea valued at Rs. 1,621.85 million, 8.64 million kgs of tea bags, valued at Rs. 2.,484.36 million and 21.70 million kgs of instant tea valued at Rs. 5,057.60 million.

Tea is one of India's major export items and India should do all it can to recover the markets being cornered by its rivals, Sri Lanka, Kenya and China and the newly-emerging tea producer, Vietnam. Tea planters and blenders would do well to ensure that they cut down costs to compete with rivals in the global, as well as the domestic market.

Coffee

Coffee, described as the "wonderful stimulant," which goes from India among other countries to Italy, Russia, Germany, Spain, Slovania and Ukraine, has been facing troubled times in recent years. Not only have the prices in the international market been going down, but exports have also declined steeply to Rs. 10,822.23 million in 2003-2004 from Rs. 17,320.4 million in 1998-99. The decline continued in 2004-05 with exports during the year going down to Rs. 10,690.77 million.

However, there are now signals of a revival in the international coffee market with exports touching Rs. 15,886.85 million in 2005-06 and Rs. 2007.90 million in 2006-07. Exports again went up to Rs. 2,046 million in 2007-08 and Rs. 2,242.64 million in 2008-09, according to official figures.

India is one of the seven major coffee producing countries, the others being Brazil, Vietnam, Indonesia, Mexico, Columbia and Guatemala. India accounts for 4.5 per cent of the world coffee production. There are over 170,000 coffee farms in nearly 900,000 acres, cultivating coffee trees, providing employment to over 6,00,000 people. Among coffee growing states, Karnataka accounts for 70 per cent of the country's total coffee production, followed by Kerala (22 per cent) and Tamil Nadu (7 per cent).

India ranks sixth in world coffee production with an annual production of about 300,000 tons. Arabica and Robusta are two main varieties grown comprising 47 per cent and 53 per cent of area respectively. Latin American countries are the lead producers of coffee and as a result, international coffee prices are vulnerable to the production trends in these countries.

Although India's share in global coffee production is less than 5 per cent, Indian coffee has created a niche for itself in the overseas market, particularly in the case of Robustas, which are preferred for their good blending qualities. Indian Arabica too is well received.

Indian coffee has been described as the most extra-ordinary of beverages, offering intriguing subtlety and stimulating intensity. India is the only country that grows all of its coffee under shade. Typically mild and not too acidic, these coffees possess an exotic taste and a fine aroma. In India, coffee is cultivated under a well-defined two-tier mixed shade canopy, comprising evergreen leguminous trees.

Italy, with imports of 50,802 tons of coffee in 2008-09, was the largest market for Indian coffee. The Russian Federation came next, followed by Germany, Belgium, Spain, Ukraine, Finland, Jordon, Croatia and Slovenia. Other major markets were Greece, France, Malaysia, Kuwait and Switzerland. It is hoped that the measures like re-plantation and rejuvenation, and the special package for coffee growers would help increase production as also the exportable surplus. It would also enable the Indian coffee industry to compete with its rivals thereby helping the growth in coffee exports. While India imported tea, although one-tenth of its exports in value terms, it has not been importing coffee.

Rubber

Rubber, used in the production of a host of products, including tyres and tubes for automobiles and cycles, is one of the commodities in which the export of value-added products have shown good growth. The value of rubber products exported has gone up more than fourteen-fold from Rs. 2,630.5 million in 1991 to Rs. 36,062.3 million in 2004-05. The exports went up further to Rs. 38,328.7 million in 2005-06.

India's export of natural rubber has been declining over the years. India exported 25,090 tons of natural rubber in

2009-10 as against 46,926 tons in the previous year. Her exports in 2006-07 was of the order of 56,545 tons. In 2005-06, a total of 73,830 tons of natural rubber was exported compared to 46,150 tons in the previous year. The exports reached their peak of 75,905 tons in 2003-04. India has not been exporting synthetic rubber. On the other hand, it has been importing it in huge quantities.

India is the fourth largest producer of natural rubber in the world, next only to Thailand, Indonesia and Malaysia, sharing about 9 per cent of total world rubber production. India produced 772,000 tons of natural rubber in 2005 against 2,833,000 tons of Thailand, 2,271,000 tons of Indonesia and 1,126,000 tons of Malaysia, according to the Rubber Board.

Besides natural rubber, India produced 97,634 tons of synthetic rubber and 72,905 tons of reclaimed rubber in 2005-06. The production of rubber, including synthetic rubber, was a high of 938,143 tons in 2009-10.

In 2005-06, of the total exports of 73,830 tons of rubber, 35,187 tons was of RSS grades, 24,153 tons in the form of latex concentrates, while 13,396 tons of solid block rubber and the remaining in RSS. The exports fetched the country Rs. 4,582 million.

Imports of rubber have gone up from 19,770 tons in 1996-97 to 170,679 tons in 2009-10. Imports in 2004-05 was 45,285 tons. In spite of the demand of the Automotive Tyre Manufacturers' Association (ATMA), the Government has ruled out any ban on rubber export. China was the biggest market for Indian rubber, importing 26,521 tons, valued at Rs.1,692 million in 2005-06, followed by Sri Lanka, Malaysia, Germany, Belgium and Turkey. Other major markets were Vietnam, the UK, the USA, Spain, Korea and Nepal, all importing more than a thousand tons.

Exports of rubber manufactured products, excepting footwear, during 2005-06 were of the order of Rs. 40,138.75 million. The exports included auto tyres and tubes, including re-treading material, belting, cycle tyres and tubes, hoses, hygienic medical and surgical articles, including gloves, rubber coats and aprons for textile industry, rubber sheeting and other articles.

The USA was the largest importer of rubber products, importing from India rubber goods of the value of Rs. 4,089.80 million in 2004-05. The UAE came next with imports valued at Rs. 2,351.97 million. They were followed by Germany, Pakistan, Philippines and the UK. Other major markets for rubber goods included Australia, Iran, Saudi Arabia, Singapore, France, Spain, Afghanistan, Belgium, Malaysia and Hong Kong.

Rubber products from India went to far off Latin American countries too. Among them Peru, Chile, Brazil, Columbia, Venezuela and Argentina imported more than Rs.100 million worth each. In Africa, the major markets in 2004-05 were Nigeria, South Africa, Kenya, Ghana, Uganda, Sudan and Cote d' Ivore.

Besides Pakistan, other neighbouring countries, which imported rubber goods in substantial quantities were Bangladesh, Afghanistan, Sri Lanka, Nepal and Myanmar.

In footwear, India produces a scintillating range that is specially designed for fashion conscious women of today, as also enchanting collection of footwear for men with distinguished taste. The footwear come in a variety of individual designs and colour.

Footwear of rubber and canvas is being imported from India by more than 100 countries. The United Kingdom was India's biggest market for rubber footwear, followed by United States, Italy, Germany, France, Spain and the UAE.

In spite of being the fourth largest producer of natural rubber, imports of the commodity by India surged to 170,048 tons in the year-ended March 31, 2010, from 77,762 tons a year earlier, according to the Rubber Board. Tyre manufacturers may boost imports to 200,000 tons in 2010-11.

8
Manufactured Goods

Manufactured goods occupy a singular position in India's foreign trade with 74 per cent share in the country's total exports. Within manufacturing, the high performers have been engineering goods (mainly manufactures of metals, machinery and instrument, transport equipment, primary and semi-finished iron and steel and non-ferrous metal). Other items were gems and jewelry, chemicals and related products (including basic chemicals, pharmaceuticals and cosmetics and toiletries), plastics, linoleum, rubber, leather and glass. Engineering goods are being given a separate treatment.

Tobacco

India is the third largest producer and the eighth largest exporter of tobacco and tobacco products in the world, contributing 10 per cent of total excise duty collected by the government, besides state levies such as octroi duty and luxury taxes. Still, tobacco is not a favoured industry with the government, which has been imposing curbs on its domestic consumption, obviously for reasons of its being deleterious to health.

Endowed with rich agro-climatic attributes, like fertile soil, plentiful rainfall and ample sunshine, India produces various types of tobacco, like FCV traditional, FCV (Mysore), FCV (NLS), Burley, dark cigarette tobacco, SC Burley tobacco, Lalchopadia, Judi, Rustica and others, all of which are exported. On an average, India produces 10 million kg of Burley tobacco.

In spite of the global economic recession, India's tobacco exports have been bullish and strong. Exports of tobacco and tobacco products increased by about 68 per cent to Rs. 33,880 million in 2008-09 over the previous year. After receiving a setback in 2001-02, India's exports of tobacco (both manufactured and un-manufactured) have been rising year after year, going up to Rs. 20,209.3 million in 2007-08, compared to Rs. 8,885.2 million in 2001-02. Of the total exports in 2008-09, un-manufactured tobacco fetched Rs. 27,132 million, while tobacco products netted Rs. 6751.5 million. The growth over the years has been significant, with exports in the year 1960-61 being worth only Rs. 160 million.

*Among products, chewing tobacco (**zarda**) occupied the top position with exports valued at Rs. 2.520.5 million in 2007-08, followed by cigarettes at Rs. 1,431.6 million. Exports of '**hooka**' tobacco paste, together with cut tobacco, amounted to Rs. 467.8 million and '**bides**' Rs. 445.7 million. Still, the export of value added tobacco was low, compared to un-manufactured tobacco.*

Currently, Indian tobacco is being exported to more than 80 countries spread over all continents. Top multinational cigarette companies, like BAT, Philip Morris, R J Rayeolds, SETTA, Imperial, and many government monopoly companies all over the world are importing Indian tobacco, either directly or indirectly. Efforts are underway to expand cultivation to new areas to meet the growing export demand.

Although, the export of tobacco products in 2004-05 was just 28.87 per cent of the total exports of tobacco and tobacco products, as against 29.78 per cent in the previous year, the proportion has generally shown a rising trend. Tobacco products constituted barely 2.2 per cent of the overall exports of tobacco in 1974-75. The exports of value-added tobacco products have shown a rising trend since 1998-99, when it was 21.29 per cent of overall tobacco exports. In value terms, exports of products in 1998-99 was Rs. 1,717 million in total exports of Rs. 8,061.9 million. It went up from Rs. 1,854.5 million in 1999-2000, to Rs. 2,263.4 million in 2000-01 and further to Rs. 2,856.3 million in 2001-02.

The rising trend was maintained when tobacco products exports stood at Rs. 3,253.30 million in 2002-03 out of total tobacco exports of Rs. 10,959.5 million. In 2003-04, tobacco products exports were of the order of Rs. 3,501.5 million out of a total tobacco export of Rs. 11,756.3 million. In 2004-05, tobacco products exports rose further to Rs. 3,932 million out of total tobacco exports of Rs. 13,621.8 million.

*Among tobacco products, chewing tobacco (*zarda*) occupied the top position with an export of 8,383 tons valued at Rs. 2,520.6 million in 2007-08, replacing cigarettes, which held the top position in 2004-05 with an export of Rs. 1,431.6 million. However, compared to Rs. 1551.80 million in 2004-05, there was a decline in cigarette exports in 2007-08, the latest period for which disaggregated figures are available.*

Nearly 4,695 tons of cut tobacco, worth Rs. 576.7 million was exported in 2007-08 and 9,577 tons of hookah *tobacco paste valued at Rs. 467.8 million.* Bidis *followed with an export of Rs. 445.7 million in 2007-08. The growth is noticeable as* bidi *export had slumped to Rs. 32.90 million in 2005-06. Exports of* Hookah *tobacco paste was Rs. 467.6 million 207-08. Snuff, although its exports both in quantity and value terms was negligible, showed a growth of 397.05 per cent to Rs.16.9 million from Rs. 3.4 million in 2004-05.*

*The USA was the largest market for cigarettes in 2004-05 (Rs. 584.45 million), The UAE for '*bidis*' (Rs. 208.66 million), chewing tobacco (Rs. 767.21 million) and cut tobacco (Rs. 140.42 million), while Saudi Arabia happened to be the largest market for '*Hooka*' tobacco (Rs. 388.63 million). Other major markets for cigarettes were the UAE, Iraq, Egypt, and Panama. For 'bidis', besides the UAE, the other markets were Yemen, Afghanistan, Singapore and Iran. Even the United States bought '*bidis*' worth Rs. 8.03 million. For '*hooka*' tobacco paste, besides Saudi Arabia, other markets were Yemen and*

Tunisia. For chewing tobacco, the other major markets were Iran, the UK, and Yemen. For cut tobacco, besides the UAE, Nigeria and the USA were the other two markets.

As for un-manufactured tobacco, Belgium was the largest market in 2008-09, importing 38,740 tons worth Rs. 6,624.5 million, taking a lead over Russia, which was the largest market in 2004-05, importing Rs. 1,624.24 million worth. Belgium was the second largest market in 2004-05, importing Rs. 1,173.79 million worth, followed by United Kingdom, Egypt and Ukraine.

North Korea was another country that showed good growth. Germany, the Netherlands, France and South Africa, although major markets for un-manufactured tobacco, showed heavy declines in 2004-05. In South and South-East Asia, Vietnam, DPR Korea, Malaysia, Singapore and Nepal were emerging as major markets.

Exports assume importance in the context of curbs on domestic consumption. The latest attempt to curb consumption is the Tobacco Products (Prohibition of Advertisement and Regulation of Trade and Commerce, Production, Supply and Distribution) Act, 2003. The act imposes restrictions on the advertisement of tobacco products, the sale of tobacco products to minors, labelling on packaging and a plethora of measures all aimed at curtailing tobacco consumption.

India needs to maintain the growth in its exports of products, rather than un-manufactured tobacco, if exports are to bring greater realization in value terms. In products, the largest potential for a developing market is in cigarettes. Chewing tobacco and '**zarda**' *too have a good potential, at least in countries with a good proportion of Indian population. The country should set up production facilities, if necessary, in collaboration with multinationals, who are currently depending on imports of un-manufactured tobacco from India. Only by exporting high value tobacco products can India realize export proceeds that are due to the country and help benefit the farmers, who labour and toil to produce it.*

Gems and Jewelry

India, long known for its expertise in cutting and polishing diamonds, is turning to the manufacture of gold jewelry, exports of diamonds having reached a saturation point. Exports of cut and polished diamonds netted Rs. 500,740 million, which formed 72.75 per cent of total exports of gem and jewelry sector at Rs. 686,460 million in 2004-05, according to figures available from Gem and Jewelry Export Promotion Council (GJEPC).

Over the last 40 years, India has risen to the top of the diamond cutting business. Nine out of ten rough diamonds are cut and polished and re-exported from India. This leaves little room for growth unless the industry can move to high-value diamonds.

The Gem and Jewelry sector is India's leading foreign exchange earner. The industry has accounted for 18.33 per cent, nearly one fifth of India's total exports for the year 2004-05. There has been a remarkable growth in exports in dollar terms from US $28 million in 1966-67 to over US $ 12 billion in 2003-04. The exports swelled further to US $15.67 billion in 2004-05 and to US $ 16.7 billion in 2005-06. In rupee terms, exports in 2005-06 were valued at Rs. 688,301 million according to provisional figures available from GJKEPC. In 2008-09, exports of gem and jewelry aggregated Rs. 1,285,750 million, according to figures available with the Director General Commercial Intelligence and Statistics (DGCI&S). The exports further swelled to 1,372,003 million in 2009-10, according to DGCI&S provisional figures. The exports of precious, semi-precious stones and gold and silver amounted to Rs.1,066,507 million.

As stated earlier, the major contributor to the growth in exports was cut and polished diamonds (CPD). Exports of CPD were valued at US $11,182 million in 2004-05 compared to US $8,627.48 million in the previous year. It is noteworthy, *however, that total imports of diamonds by India in 2004-05 were valued at US $7,646.7 million. The net value addition was thus US $3,535.3 million. The exports of diamonds in 2005-06 was US $11,860.49 million.*

Exports of gold jewelry showed a growth of 34.76 per cent in dollar terms in 2004-05 over the previous year. Gold jewelry exports went up to US $3,813 million in 2004-05 from US $2,681 million in the previous year. The exports had more than doubled in two years considering that they were of the order of US $1,513 million in 2002-03. In 2005-06, however, exports of gold jewelry showed a nominal growth of 1.28 per cent to 3,861.57 million. Coloured gem stones grew by 21.5 per cent to US $233.32 million in 2005-06 compared to 192.75 million in 2004-05, according to figures available from the GJEPC.

Indian jewelers have discovered that it is profitable to enter gold jewelry exports, where they had the same advantages—cheap and highly-skilled labour. So far gold jewelry was being sold mainly to buyers within the country. One big reason was that the craftsmen were trained in the traditional style of jewelry-making, whereas markets like the US demanded simple but stylish ornaments.

Things have been made easy for jewelers to enter the field of gold ornaments. All restrictions on gold import have been eased and jewelry manufacturing equipment attract lower rates of duty, thanks to the general reduction in tariffs. Imports of gold and silver have gone up. Diamond merchants, are also trying to enter the diamond studded branded jewelry segment. Indian merchants plan to brand their jewelry and create a market for these in India and abroad.

The United States, Japan, Belgium, Israel and Hong Kong constituted major gem and jewelry markets for India. The United States imported from India in 2004-05 cut and polished diamonds worth US $2,584.76 million, gold jewelry worth US $1,348.78 million and coloured gem stones worth US $.88.35 million. Imports of cut & polished diamonds by the

USA rose to US $2,858.10 million in 2005-06, of gold jewelry to US $1,711.3 million and coloured gem stones to US $100.50 million.

In cut and polished diamonds Hong Kong with imports from India worth US $3,042.11 million in 2004-05 and US $3,432.03 million in 2005-06 surpassed the United States in the import of the item from India. The UAE with imports worth US $1,845 million in 2004-05 came next, followed by Belgium, Japan, Thailand and Switzerland. Besides, the United States, other leading markets for gold jewelry in 2004-05 were the UAE, the UK, Hong Kong, Kuwait, Belgium, Bahrain and Germany.

In coloured gem stones, Thailand came next to the USA, importing from India US $26.53 million worth in 2004-05. It was followed by Japan, Germany, Italy, Switzerland, France and the UK. In pearls and synthetic stones, total exports were around US $8 million and market for both needed to be cultivated.

A number of measures to achieve the objective of making India a gems and jewelry hub of the world were announced in the annual supplement to the Foreign Trade Policy in April 2006. The measures include allowing import of precious metal scrap and used jewelry for melting, refining and re-export; permission for export of jewelry on consignment basis; permission to export polished, precious and semi-precious stones for treatment abroad and re-import in order to enhance the quality and afford high value in the international market. The value addition norms have been reduced due to the increase in prices of gold and silver in international market.

The Gem and Jewelry Export Promotion Council is making all out efforts to enhance exports. It is hoped that with the efforts of the Council, the industry's expectations in the field of exports would be fulfilled.

Gold and Silver

In 2008-09, India imported gold of the value of Rs. 953,238 million, double the value imported in 2005-06, according to figures available from the DGCI&S. The larger imports are obviously due to the industry seeking to enhance the production and export of gold jewelry.

India imported silver worth Rs. 94,625.87 million in 2008-09 compared to Rs. 21,571.09 million in 2005-06.

South Africa was one of the main sources of gold imports by India. Other major sources were Hong Kong, Indonesia, France, Germany, Luxemburg and Singapore. Main sources for the import of silver by India were the United Kingdom, the UAE, Switzerland and Uzbekistan.

Leather

Leather industry occupies a place of prominence in India, with annual production of over US$ 4 billion, 50 per cent of which constitutes exports. The industry provides employment to a workforce of about 2.50 million, 30 per cent of whom are women. The composition of export of leather and leather products has undergone a structural change over the past five decades—from an exporter of raw material, India has become an exporter of value added products in the nineties. India accounts for a share of 2.56 per cent in the global leather trade and value-added finished products presently constitute 80 per cent of total exports of the industry, according to the Council for Leather Exports (CLE). Despite registering high growth, leather and leather goods exports were witnessing a fall owing to appreciation of the European currency, which had appreciated from Rs. 65 per Euro to about Rs. 56-57 a Euro.

Leather comprises raw hides and skin, finished leather, leather goods, leather garments, footwear of leather, footwear components and saddlery and harness. Leather exports have gone up to Rs. 169,176.53 million (provisional) in 2009-10, from Rs. 163,507.77 million in the previous year. While the value of exports of finished leather, leather goods, leather footwear components and saddlery and harness declined in 2008-09, leather garments, footwear of leather witnessed an increase in exports.

Finished leather exports declined to Rs. 29,677.48 million in 2009-10 from Rs. 30,970.70 million in the previous year and leather goods to Rs. 35,867.98 million from Rs. 40,172.54 million.

Leather exports have been a high growth item for India. There has been good growth in exports of leather, which includes finished leather, leather goods, leather garments, footwear of leather, leather footwear components and saddlery and harness.

In 2004-05, exports of finished leather and other leather items were of the value of Rs. 106,911.95 million, registering a growth of 4.97 per cent over Rs. 101,848.94 million in the previous year, according to figures available from CLE.

However, in 2009-10, exports of leather and leather goods witnessed a fall owing to appreciation of the European currency. Thus, as per CLE data, the net exports of leather and leather goods for the period April-March 2009-10 stood at US $3,400.97 million, which was 5.1 per cent down, as compared to the same period last year, which recorded US $3,599.46 million.

In 2004-05, the performance of the sector exceeded the target in all categories except leather garments and saddlery and harness. The export of finished leather went up to US$577 million as against a target of US $520 million, of leather footwear, including leather uppers, to US $766 million as against a target of US $760 million, of leather goods to US $568 million as against a target of US $515 million. In the case of leather garments as against a target of US $325 million, the achievement was only US $319 million and in the case of saddlery and harness, it was US $60 million as against a target of US $65 million. In non-leather footwear, included by CLE in leather exports, the achievement was only US $90 million, as against a target of US $99 million. The overall achievement was US $2,379 million against the target of US $2,284 million.

In recent years, China has been providing heavy competition to India, having developed high quality leather from pig's skin as against those of sheep and goat used in India, which is 50 per cent costlier, according to CLE.

The Indian leather industry is primarily in the organized sector. The main production units are located at Ambur, Ranipet, Vaniyambadi, Trichur and Dindigul in Tamil Nadu; Kolkata in West Bengal, Kanpur, Agra and Noida in Uttar Pradesh; Jallandhar in Punjab; Bangalur in Karnataka and Hyderabad in Andhra Pradesh; Haryana and Delhi. Tamil Nadu is the biggest leather exporter in the country with the south accounting for nearly 43 per cent of the country's share. India has the largest livestock in the world with 21 per cent of large animals and 11 per cent of small animals. Ten per cent of the global leather requirement is sourced from India, says CLE.

Leather goods, which have shown a growth of 3.08 per cent in 2004-05, includes a number of popular items, like gloves and ladies hand bag. Some new items have also come in, such as sofa covers, car seat covers and upholstery. Calcutta is the seat of leather goods industry with 70 per cent of goods being manufactured there, according to CLE.

The growth in footwear of leather, including leather uppers, in 2004-05 was 4.77 per cent with exports of Rs. 34,390.32 million against Rs. 32,823.70 million in the previous year. Saddlery and harness showed a growth of 10.64 per cent, with its exports going up to Rs. 2,679.90 million in 2004-05 from Rs. 2,422.25 million in the previous year.

Germany with imports worth Rs. 15,127.48 million in 2004-05 happened to be the topmost buyer of India's finished leather, followed by the UK Rs. 13,443 million, the USA Rs. 12,566 million and Italy Rs. 10,900 million.

Hong Kong, Spain, France, the Netherlands, the UAE, Portugal, Australia, Belgium, Republic of Korea, Denmark and

Canada, all with imports worth over Rs. 1,000 million in 2004-05 were other major markets for Indian leather.

Germany showed preference for value-added products, importing leather goods worth Rs. 4,023.99 million, leather garments worth Rs. 2,520.56 million, footwear of leather worth Rs. 5,788.31 million, leather footwear components worth Rs. 1,268.79 million and saddlery and harness worth Rs.492.44 million. The UK, the second largest market for Indian leather, imported leather goods worth Rs. 3,943.14 million, leather garments worth Rs. 990.48 million, leather footwear worth Rs. 6,906.39 million, leather footwear components worth Rs. 1,028.31 million and saddlery and harness worth Rs. 331.66 million.

In the case of the USA and the UK, as also to some extent France, their imports of finished leather was low, but that of other items, high. The United States imported in 2004-05, leather goods worth Rs. 5,072.06 million, leather garments worth Rs. 2,092.31 million, footwear of leather worth Rs. 4,180.7 million and saddlery and harness worth Rs. 499.69 million.

Italy, another major market for Indian leather, imported finished leather worth Rs. 2,994.06 million, leather goods worth Rs. 1,525.19 million, leather garments worth Rs. 2,346.14 million, footwear of leather worth Rs. 2,748.45 million and leather footwear components worth Rs. 1,529.3 million. France, yet another major market for Indian leather, imported in 2004-05 finished leather from India worth Rs. 732.98 million, leather goods worth Rs. 1,279.75 million, leather garments worth Rs. 1,109.5 million, footwear of leather worth Rs. 1,933.73 million and saddlery and harness worth Rs. 248.73 million.

China and Hong Kong, both India's competitors in leather in the international market, imported mainly finished leather. Besides China and Hong Kong other major markets for India's leather included Spain, Portugal, Italy, Brazil and Argentina.

With the help and support of CLE and policy support of the Government, there is good scope for widening the country's export market in leather. One area, which has quite a lot of potential is Eastern Europe. There is need for India to increase the production of value-added products as the market in future is going to be for upper-end products. To be able to effectively compete with its rivals, it is necessary for Indian manufacturers to cut down cost and to develop ever-new, attractive and colourful materials to cater to the needs of the European and US markets, which are likely to expand in the years to come.

Footwear

India is a major producer of footwear, particularly of leather, where it ranks next only to China. Lately, however, China has reportedly been facing serious problems due to rising labour costs and currency appreciation. Chinese products, which were 10 per cent cheaper, compared to Indian, are no longer so. Most of the global footwear dealers, particularly European, who were sourcing from China, have now turned to India.

The estimated annual footwear production capacity of India has been 2,065 million pairs of different categories of footwear, which works out to 13 per cent of global footwear production of 16 billion pairs. India produces 909 million pairs of leather footwear, 100 million pairs of leather shoe uppers and 1056 million pairs of non-leather footwear.

Footwear export surged to Rs. 68,768.05 million in 2008-09 from Rs. 26,285.93 million in 1999-2000 registering a growth of 161 per cent in a decade. Exports registered constant rise in terms of rupee, although in 2002-03 growth was a measly 1.82 per cent, according to figures available from DGCI&S. In dollar terms, however, there was a 4.59 per cent decline in 2002-03, when exports went down to US $ 625.25 million from US $ 655.35 million, as per DGCI&S figures.

Footwear exports included rubber footwear and footwear components, mostly shoe uppers. With the increase in the export of leather footwear, leather footwear components, no doubt registered a decline. Footwear components exports declined to an estimated Rs. 3956.19 million in 2009-10 from Rs. 9.320.62 million in 1999-2000.

In dollar terms, exports of footwear increased from US $ 606 million in 1999-2000 to US $1,507.51 million in 2009-10 giving it a share of 44.33 per cent in total exports from the leather sector.

Footwear of leather went to more than 148 countries from India. During 2009-10, the main markets for Indian footwear were the UK (US $296.45 million) with a share of 19.66 per cent, Germany (US $224.27 million) 14.88 per cent, Italy (US $209.95 million) 13.93 percent, France (US $145.44 million) 9.58 per cent, the USA (US $123 million) 8.20 per cent, Spain (US $95.99 million) 6.37 per cent, the Netherlands (US $65.13 million) 4.32 per cent, UAE (US $39.61 million) 2.63 per cent, Portugal (US $22.63 million) 1.5 per cent and Denmark (US $17.02 million) 1.13 per cent, accounting for 82.20 per cent in India's total footwear exports, according to DGCI&S figures.

In leather footwear components, the growth was 16.96 per cent in 2004-05 with exports of Rs. 8,052.21 million against Rs. 6,884.42 million in the previous year. The growth in 2004-05 was meaningless, considering that footwear component exports stood at Rs. 11,156.87 million in 2001-02. The decline has been attributed to the preference by European footwear manufacturers for full shoes to offset rising labour costs. Consequently, the export of shoe uppers have been adversely impacted. In general too, the pattern of exports is expected to shift to value-added products.

Although low in value terms, rubber footwear exports galloped 143.75 per cent to Rs. 3,170.55 million in 2003-04 from Rs. 1,300.75 million in the previous year. The exports went up further to Rs. 3,315.04 million in 2004-05, but declined to Rs. 2,428.31 million in 2005-06. Rubber footwear exports declined further to Rs. 2000.33 million in 2008-09 and is estimated to have gone up marginally to Rs. 2087.99 million in 2009-10, according to provisional figures available from DGCI&S.

India produces a scintillating range of rubber footwear, that is specially designed for fashion conscious women of today, as also enchanting collection of footwear for men with distinguished taste. The footwear come in a variety of individual designs and colour.

The Northern Indian state of Punjab produces gorgeous100 per cent hand-crafted and hand-stitched leather slip-ons (jooti) with amazing pink and gold beadwork and sequin work, as also with lovely hand embroidered toe curl. Some of these are replicas of shoes worn by kings in India, which were set in real gold or silver thread and adorned with precious stones.

Footwear exported from India include dress shoes, casuals, moccasins, sports sandals, ballerinas, boots and chappals made of rubber, plastic, PVC and other materials. Major MNC brands sourced from India include ACME, Clarks, Colehann, Deichmann Florsheim, Hasley, Marks and Spencer, Nike, Reebok, Salamander and Bally. MNC brands sold in India include Clarks, Florshiem, Lloyd, Marks and Spencer, Nike and Reebok. Indian brands sold in India include Bata, Liberty, Lakhani, Metro and Action.

There are new emerging possibilities for footwear export as according to a research report, it is projected to grow at a CAGR of nearly 20 per cent between 2008-09 and 2010-11. This would amount to over 60 per cent of total leather export from India. Easy availability of skilled manpower and relatively much lower cost are expected to keep the demand for Indian footwear buoyant in the near future.

In order to reduce the impact of the economic recession on the footwear market, India is trying to diversify its footwear market from its present potential export markets to new avenues. As of now most of the Indian export is concentrated in the EU and the United Stated. The country is, therefore, targeting the Middle East region to sell leather goods and footwear with a view to further explore the possibilities of enhancing footwear export to the potential market. The Leather Council has, therefore, lent emphasis on undertaking aggressive market development activities in the Middle East region.

Among the Middle East countries, Saudi Arabia and Jordon import significant volume of leather and leather products from the global market. Their total global imports are around US $414 million, while India is exporting to them only about US $16 million, which works out to a share of 3.88 per cent. There is, therefore, a great scope of enhancing India's market share in these countries.

Further, Special Economic Zone (SEZ) Park is being set up for the footwear sector on a land measuring 150 acres in Sipcot industrial Estate in Tamil Nadu, 34 kms from Chennai. The Park is being set up on global standards with adequate infrastructure facilities. Another SEZ for leather products is also underway in 260 acres at Ranipet in Tamil Nadu, besides Special Integrated Leather Parks in different parts of the country.

Footwear is the engine of growth of the leather industry, currently accounting for an export value of US $1,212 million, holding a major share of 41 per cent in India's total leather trade. Taking this into account, the CLE has set up an ambitious target of US $4.5 billion for footwear exports from India by 2010-11, wherein the overall export of leather products will reach US $ 6.98 billion, giving the footwear section alone a share of 65 per cent in India's total leather export.

Drugs and Pharmaceuticals

India is the fourth largest producer of pharmaceuticals in terms of volume and thirteenth in terms of value of production globally. The annual turnover was around US $17 billion (over Rs. 680,000 million) during 2006-07 and was estimated to grow to Rs. 1,000,000 million in formulations and bulk drug *production in 2010. The Indian pharmaceutical industry employs around 500,000 people. It is a highly fragmented market with around 20,000 production units. The industry is capable of meeting 80 per cent of the country's drug requirements at relatively lower cost compared to international brands.*

India exports bulk drugs to more than 200 countries across the globe, including highly-regulated markets of the US, Europe, Japan and Australia. India's exports of drugs and pharmaceuticals have grown manifold during the last two decades or more. Exports have grown from Rs. 460 million in 1980-81 to Rs. 400,000 million in 2008-09. Exports stood at Rs. 143,221 million in 2003-04 and have grown to Rs. 221,157.24 million in 2005-06.

The Indian pharmaceutical industry has evolved significantly since Independence. Initially, MNCs had a near monopoly. They imported and marketed formulations in India, mainly low cost generics for the masses and also a few specialties, life-saving, high priced products. With the growth of Indian industry following the setting up of the Hindustan Antibiotics Ltd and other companies in the public and the private sectors, India has achieved global recognition as a low cost producer and supplier of quality bulk drugs and formulations in the world.

The government has in the Pharmaceutical policy 2002 abolished industrial licensing for all bulk drugs, cleared by the Drug Controller General (India) and for all intermediates and formulations, subject to stipulations laid down from time to time. Further, foreign investment up to 100 per cent is being permitted, subject to these stipulations. The steps have been taken to enable the industry face new challenges on account of liberalization of the Indian economy, globalization of the world economy and obligations undertaken by India under the WTO agreements.

The pharmaceutical industry in India today meets around 80 per cent of the country's demand for bulk drugs, drug intermediates, pharmaceutical formulations, chemicals, tablets, *capsules, orals and injectibles at a comparatively lower cost compared to international brands. India's US $3.1 billion worth pharmaceutical industry is growing at the rate of 14 per cent a year. It is one of the largest and most advanced among developing countries.*

With the imminent change in Indian patent legislation, India's more ambitious indigenous pharmaceutical companies are developing strategies to reduce their dependence on the domestic generics market. Two main business models are emerging. On the one hand, there is entry into regulated international markets with generics, formulations and specialty pharmaceuticals and on the other there is provision of contract services to the international pharmaceutical industry in the fields of contract manufacturing for marketing drugs, as well as clinical trial of supplies, synthetic chemistry for drug discovery and clinical development.

The global pharmaceutical industry, beleaguered with ever-increasing pressures to reduce the costs of getting new products to the market, is examining the opportunities for outsourcing to India with much interest. This is quite remarkable bearing in mind the traditional attitudes of the pharmaceutical industry, as also the fact that during the past decades Indian generic companies have 'reverse engineered' their innovator products to sell them in unregulated markets for a fraction of the price. A growing list of international pharmaceutical companies that include a majority of the world's top 10 companies, is accessing pharmaceutical services from India. This is being conducted via outsourcing contractual arrangements with local providers, striking alliances with Indian partners and by setting up wholly-owned Indian subsidiaries.

As a consequence of thriving generics, formulation and bulk drug industry, India has developed world class synthetic chemistry skills and invested in state-of-the-art manufacturing facilities. Today, apart from the USA, India has the largest number of FDA approved pharmaceutical manufacturing plants. In comparison, India has lagged behind in developing the skills that support an innovative R&D based pharmaceutical industry. Examples of such skills are medicinal chemistry, pharmacology, proteomics, genomics, and molecular and cellular biology. India also lacks a well-funded, dynamic biomedical academic community that is essential for pharmaceutical innovation.

Notwithstanding these shortfalls, India has compelling attractions for the global pharmaceutical industry, namely, large English-speaking population, cost-effective graduate workforce with degrees in sciences, IT and medicine, large, heterogeneous, Caucasian population, proven track record in providing outsourced IT services to world beating standards. The scientific and technical workforce in India has three million individuals. In addition, there are one million graduate engineers and 0.8 million postgraduate scientists. The cost of pre-clinical discovery in India is estimated to be one-fifth of what it is in advanced countries.

Besides exports, India also imported medicinal and pharmaceutical products. China exported to India medicinal and pharmaceutical products worth Rs. 15,786.64 million in 2005-06, emerging as the largest exporter of the items to India. Other major exporters of products to India were Switzerland (Rs. 5,478 million), the USA (Rs. 4,257.36 million), Germany (2,788.67 million), Denmark (Rs. 1,735.37 million), Italy (Rs. 1,708.61 million), the UK (Rs. 1336.88 million), Sri Lanka (Rs. 1,018.36 million) and the Netherlands (Rs. 941.21 million).

The United States has been the largest importer of drugs, pharmaceuticals and fine chemicals from India, with imports worth Rs. 71,032.2 million in 2008-09 compared to Rs. 31,684 million in 2005-06. The United States was followed by Russia Germany, the UK, South Africa. Canada, Brazil, and Nigeria each with imports worth more than Rs. 10,000 million. They were followed by Ukraine, Israel, the Netherlands, Spain, Turkey, China, Kenya, Vietnam, Belgium, Italy and Mexico with imports worth more than Rs. 5,000 million.

Other major importers of Indian drugs and pharmaceuticals with imports above Rs. 1,000 million each in 2004-05 and 2005-06 were Israel, Belgium, Malaysia, Australia, Argentina, Afghanistan, France and the Philippines.

Nearer home, besides Afghanistan, exports to Bangladesh rose to Rs. 2,433 million in 2004-05 and further to Rs. 2886.47 million in 2005-06 from Rs. 1916.57 million in 2003-04, to Pakistan it jumped to Rs. 2,586.96 million in 2004-05 from Rs. 1158.51 million in 2003-04 and to Sri Lanka it went up to Rs. 2,763.39 million in 2004-05 and further to Rs. 3,072.56 million in 2005-06 from Rs. 2,311 million in 2003-04. In the case of Myanmar, it was a lowly Rs. 971.05 million in 2004-05, but rose to Rs. 1170.10 million in 2005-06.

Besides Argentina and Brazil, Indian drug industry has penetrated into other Latin American countries too, with exports to Columbia worth Rs. 1,637.42 million in 2005-06, Venezuela Rs. 719.85 million, Peru Rs. 637.19 million, Chile Rs. 720.84 million, Uruguay Rs. 314.29 million, Guyana Rs. 126.92 million, Honduras Rs. 291.52 million, Guatemala Rs. 376.27 million. Although other Latin American countries, like Bolivia, El Salvador, Guyana, Ecuador, Paraguay, imported drugs below Rs. 100 million worth in 2004-05, their imports in 2005-06 were much more, which shows that there are good prospects for increasing exports to these countries.

Among African countries too, besides Nigeria and South Africa, others having sizeable imports of drugs and pharmaceuticals from India in 2004-05 and 2005-06 were Kenya (Rs. 1,277.14. million and Rs. 1,889.85 million), Ghana (Rs. 1,151.16 million and Rs. 1,597 million) and Uganda (Rs. 914.50 million and Rs. 1,193.74 million). Several other countries, like Algeria, Egypt, Ethiopia, Tanzania and Sudan imported drugs and pharmaceuticals from India worth over Rs. 500 million each in 2004-05. Their imports in 2005-06 crossed Rs. 1,000 million in the case of two of them. Imports by Morocco and Senegal were between Rs. 100 million and Rs. 500 million. Only in the cases of Libya, Namibia and

Seychelles imports were less than Rs. 100 million in 2004-05. However, imports by Namibia and Morocco went up to Rs. 265.95 million and Rs. 197.55 million respectively in 2005-06. Libya too crossed the Rs. 100 million mark, importing drugs, pharmaceutical and fine chemicals worth Rs. 101.41 million in 2005-06.

A lot of promotional work is needed in the case of CIS countries as with the exception of Ukraine (Rs. 3,366.76 million) and Kazakhstan (Rs. 702.2 million). India's exports to the region was rather poor and given the cordial relations that India has been having with the region, there is ample scope for promoting our exports.

In general, however, exports of drugs and pharmaceuticals show a great deal of promise. As things stand, China is not a competitor, but rather a market for India's drugs, pharmaceuticals and fine chemicals. As a competitor, China is difficult to deal with. With emphasis on R&D in the industry, which the government has been promoting, it is hoped that the industry would expand production, promote export of quality drugs and emerge as one of the front ranking leaders in the field.

India is poised to offer the global pharmaceutical industry high quality and cost-effective contract services to support drug discovery, clinical trial, conduct data management and manufacturing. There is already a proven track record for some of these services and an enthusiasm to expand into services at the higher end of the value chain. Once India demonstrates her intent to uphold international intellectual property laws with high ethical standards, the flood gates will open and an increasing number of international pharmaceutical companies will seek to establish outsourcing arrangements in a variety of forms.

As the sector matures, the prime driver for outsourcing will change from cost saving to the quest for high quality and speed. With skills developed by the Indian workforce, pharmaceutical services industry will help India's more ambitious pharmaceutical companies to fulfill their aspirations of becoming players in the global pharmaceutical industry.

Cosmetics and Toiletries

Cosmetics and toiletries are fast-growing export items for India. In a decade since 1989-90, their exports have risen several fold, going up from Rs. 7,061.03 million in 1998-99 to Rs. 44,414.01 million in 2008-09. The exports were Rs. 16,248.15 million in 2004-05 and went up to Rs. 22,036.71 million in 2005-06, according to figures available from DGCI&S.

The high growth has been promoted by herbal products in their preparation, which have attracted a great deal of attraction even in highly-advanced countries, like the United States.

The exports include such diverse products as toothpaste and tooth brush, shaving creams, perfumes, nail polish, lipstick, face packs of basil, sandal, almond, apricot, fruits, anti-tan fairness glow face packs and henna hair oil. They also include herbal cosmetics like body moisturizers, skincare cream, fairness creams, hair shampoo, facial scrubs and hair oils. Cosmetics and toiletries are classified under HS code 33 and all items are under OGL. Soaps and detergents are the major segments of the industry and both are de-licensed.

A host of companies, led by Dabur, Baidyanath and Zandu, have contributed to the growth in exports of cosmetics and toiletries. They use herbal products, like ***haldi*** *(turmeric), lemon, sandal, rose, aloe vera, camphor,* ***tulsi, madhu*** *(honey), almond and* ***amla*** *in their beauty cream. In 2003, only 15 per cent of Dabur's sales volume was pharmaceuticals, the remaining 85 per cent were mostly non-medicinal items, such as foods and cosmetics. Some of its items in the category are Amla Hair Oil, Vatika Shampoo, Lal Dant Manjan (tooth powder). Baidyanath has massage oils. Considering the importance of the twin groups of items, Zandu has a cosmetics division.*

The recent purchase of Balsara group of companies by Dabur further shows the importance of cosmetics and toiletries. The Rs. 1,430 million deal adds seven brands to Dabur's existing portfolio. The brands are Promise, Babool, Meswak, Odonil, Odomos, Odopic and Sani Fresh. The deal includes acquisition of Balsara's three manufacturing facilities at Silva, Kanpur and Baddi. It would include Balsara's Hygiene Products, including six of the seven brands and Besta cosmetics, which owns Babool toothpaste.

The USA, which is India's the leading market in most other products, yields place to United Arab Emirates (UAE) in cosmetics and toiletries. In 2004-05, the UAE imported from India the twin products of the value of Rs. 1,898 million, which showed a decline of 44.41 per cent over Rs. 2,741 million in the previous year. The decline was steep as it was lower than Rs. 1,909 million in 2001-02. From this level, imports by the UAE rose to Rs. 2,143 million in 2002-03 and further to Rs. 2,379 million in 2003-04. Its imports in 2005-06 were a high of Rs. 3,253.96 million.

United States imported the twin commodity groups of the value of Rs. 1,706 million in 2003-04, which showed a rise of 7.4 per cent over Rs. 1,586 million in the previous year. In 2004-05, its imports from India declined to Rs. 1,469 million. In 2005-06, however, its imports shot up to Rs. 2,376.92 million.

Another leading market for India's cosmetics and toiletries is the Netherlands, which imported the twin commodity group worth Rs. 929 million in 2004-05 and Rs. 1,578.05 million in 2005-06. Its imports have been rising since 2001-02, when they stood at Rs. 265 million. Next comes Saudi Arabia, with imports worth Rs. 804 million in 2004-05, which shows a rise of 117.29 per cent over Rs. 370 million in 2001-02. Its imports in 2005-06 rose to Rs. 993.13 million. Saudi Arabia was followed by Germany, whose imports during 2004-05 were of the value of Rs.660 million, which showed a rise of 207 per cent over Rs. 215 million in 2001-02. Its imports from India, however, declined to Rs. 476.04 million in 2005-06.

Other major markets for the two commodity groups in 2004-05 and 2005-06 were Japan, Malaysia, Nepal, each with imports worth more than Rs. 500 million and Sri Lanka, the U.K., China, Indonesia, France, Italy, Singapore, South Africa, and Spain with imports between Rs. 150 million and Rs. 500 million.

In all, cosmetics and toiletries went to more than 184 countries, to most of them of very small values. Exports to Latin American countries, besides Brazil are not attractive, yet some of them show potential. These include Chile, which imported Rs. 74.93 million worth of the two commodity groups in 2003-04 as against Rs. 50.67 million worth in the previous year. Other countries are Argentina, whose imports of the category during the year grew from Rs. 17.60 million to Rs. 27.29 million, Columbia (to Rs. 29.4 million from Rs. 19.99 million) and Venezuela (to Rs. 56.5 million from Rs. 49.10 million). Brazil's imports were worth Rs. 253.53 million in 2003-04, which was a decline of 3.68 per cent over Rs. 263.23 million in 2002-03.

Besides Nigeria, some African countries too show promise, e.g. Tanzania with imports worth Rs. 82.42 million in 2003-04, up from Rs. 55.45 million in the previous year. Its imports in 2005-06 went up further to Rs. 107.69 million. In the case of Sudan, its imports in 2003-04 were worth Rs. 80.61 million, rising from Rs. 66.97 million in the previous year. Its imports in 2005-06 amounted to Rs. 78 million, a marginal decline from the level attained in 2003-04. Imports by Angola rose to Rs. 56.56 million from Rs. 48.23 million. Its imports in 2005-06, however, showed a marginal decline from 56.56 million in 2003-04. Imports by Malawi rose to Rs. 11.38 million in 2003-04 from Rs. 2.84 million in the previous year. Among neighbouring countries. Afghanistan needs to be given some attention as its imports in 2003-04 came down to Rs. 43.04 million from Rs. 58.75 million in the previous year. Its imports picked up in 2005-06, going up to Rs. 70.89 million.

There are in all 7,413 units functioning in the cosmetics and toiletries sector, of whom 1,057 are in the organized sector. The remaining 6,356 are in the small scale sector. Most of the organized sector units are located in the metropolitan cities, such as Mumbai, Calcutta, Chennai, Bangalore and Delhi. The exports are, thus, also mostly from metropolitan cities.

Considering that cosmetics and toiletries are more in use by women, special efforts should be made to woo them. Special promotional efforts should be made to popularize items of their use, say lipsticks, nail polish, shampoo, bindis, the last one more particularly among women of Indian diaspora. Since herbal cosmetics and toiletries are proving more popular even among advanced countries, which include the USA, countries of Western Europe and even Latin America, efforts should be made to popularize them further. If the right approach is made, there is scope not only of doubling, but of quadrupling the exports in less than a decade.

Sports Goods

India is one of the leading manufacturers and exporters of sports goods. It is born out of India's age-old nurtured and mastered skills in the areas of metal processing, leather crafts, wood crafts and a host of other industries, of which these items are manifest. Other major producers and exporters of sports goods are China, United Kingdom, Hong Kong, Canada, Korea, Pakistan, Taiwan and United States.

India is fast emerging as an important supplier of quality sports goods to the global markets. Indian sports goods are being exported to more than 100 countries and are in demand in some of the most developed nations of the world. The industry is rapidly embracing new technology and adapting its products to keep up with the fast changing global trends.

The exports of Indian sports goods have nearly doubled in the last decade. Exports, which stood at Rs. 2,795 million in 1999-2000, went up to Rs. 5,488.41 million in 2009-10. The exports stood at Rs. 4,596 million in 2004-05 and went up to

Rs. 5,958.71 million in 2005-06. However, exports declined to Rs. 5,868.88 million in 2008-09. The decline continued in the year that followed.

Nevertheless, with a robust and growing domestic and fast expanding overseas markets, Indian sports goods industry foresees its increasing presence in both Indian and international markets. The growth momentum of the Indian industry is supported by its huge reservoir of skilled workforce, well-established supporting and ancillary industries and availability of basic raw materials required by the industry.

The industry is rapidly embracing new technology and adapting its products to keep up with the fast changing global trends. Indian sports goods industry, which is labour intensive, with many of the units falling under the purview of small scale manufacturing units, provides employment to the weaker sections of the society as well as to a large number of women. Issues of welfare and corporate social responsibility have been given prime importance by the industry. The major manufacturing centers of the industry in India are in and around Jalandhar, Meerut, Delhi, Mumbai, Calcutta and Chennai.

The main sports equipment exported from India include inflatable balls, protective equipment for cricket, cricket bats, boxing equipment, cricket and hockey balls, bladders, fishing equipment, indoor games, including carom board and chess, protective equipment for hockey and hockey sticks. Indian manufacturers are exporting in their own brand names and as O.E.M. suppliers to international brands. Other items exported include hammocks, rackets, sports badges and insignias, toys and games, chess, T.T. equipment and boxing equipment.

The export of protective equipment for cricket went up to Rs. 362.22 million in 2009-10 from Rs. 353.37 million in the previous year, cricket bats to Rs. 489.03 million from Rs. 446.04 million, boxing equipment to Rs. 457.47 million from Rs. 383.69 million, cricket and hockey balls to Rs. 126.61 million from Rs. 111.52 million, boxing equipment to Rs. 457.47 million from Rs. 383.69 million, protective equipment for hockey Rs. 38.82 million from Rs. 32.19 million, carom board to Rs. 79.79 million from Rs. 74,50 million and hockey sticks to Rs. 36.49 million from Rs. 32.19 million.

Items, which showed decline in 2009-10 over the previous year, included inflatable balls to Rs. 1,432.34 million from 1,702.77 million, golf balls to Rs. 119.17 million from Rs. 265.77 million, protective equipment for football to Rs. 90.34 million from Rs. 105.99 million and chess sets to Rs. 42.07 million from Rs. 44.30 million.

The UK emerged as number one buyer of Indian sports goods, placing orders worth Rs. 1,800 million in 2005-06, which accounts for 40 per cent of the total sports goods' exports of Rs. 4,500 million to top 15 countries as against Rs. 1,250 million in 2004-05. Australia and the USA accounted for 20 per cent and 15 per cent of the total sports goods exports with earnings of Rs. 900 million and Rs. 607.5 million in 2005-06. Australia imported sports goods worth Rs. 650 million from India in 2005-06 and the USA worth Rs. 530 million. The sports products exported to the UK in bulk include inflatable balls, cricket equipment, boxing equipment, general exercise equipment, bladders, cricket and hockey balls, T.T equipment .and toys and games.

Germany, Italy, South Africa, and France too imported increased value of Indian sports goods in 2005-06. Germany's imports of sports goods increased to Rs. 225 million from Rs. 180 million in the previous year, Italy's to Rs. 270 million from Rs. 160 million, South Africa's to Rs. 225 million from Rs. 160 million and that of France to Rs. 180 million from Rs. 150 million.

Indian sports goods industry has acquired price competitiveness as it provides employment to the weaker sections of the society as well as to large number of women with moderate wages. This price competitiveness has given sports goods industry an edge over its competitors in the region such as Pakistan, Bangladesh and Sri Lanka.

The Indian sports goods industry exports nearly 60 per cent of its total domestic output to the sports loving countries the world over. Whereas Indian sports apparel are well recognized the world over for their excellence in quality and design, the exports of sports equipment is a high growth sector as per the assessment of ASSOCHAM. The Indian manufacturers of sports goods, both branded and unbranded, will have higher prospects in the international markets, according to Chamber's estimates.

Handicrafts

The exports of world-famous Indian handicrafts, which have a high potential, have of late faced troubled times. Exports in 2009-10, no doubt went up by 6.55 per cent over the previous year to Rs. 87,189.4 million, yet it was no where near the Rs. 172,881.4 million attained in 2006-07. The exports of handicrafts registered decline three times in the last decade. It was in 2001-02 that exports declined to Rs. 77,093.3 million from Rs. 84,901.6 million in the previous year. Next, exports went down to 140,120.5 million in 2007-08 from Rs. 172,881.4 million in 2006-07. It slid further to 81,831.2 million from 140,120.5 million in 2008-09, according to figures available from the Export Promotion Council for Handicrafts (EPCH).

Exports during 2001-02 showed a decline of 9.1 per cent after sustained growth since 1992-93, according to figures available from EPCH. The decline in 2001-2002 was obviously due to the September 11, 1991 attack on the twin towers of World Trade Organization, which affected trade worldwide.

Exports of handicrafts showed an 11.46 per cent growth to Rs. 20,543 million in 2005-06 over 16,957 million in the previous year, according to Directorate General Commercial Intelligence and Statistics (DGCI&S) of the Ministry of Commerce. According to Export Promotion Council for

Handicrafts (EPCH), however, exports grew to Rs. 145,268.5 million in 2005-06 from Rs. 130,237 million in the previous year. DGCI&S figures are much lower than those available from EPCH, as the former does not include in handicraft items like hand-printed textiles and scarves and imitation jewelry as is done by EPCH.

The country's handicrafts export contracted for eleven consecutive months from October 2008 on account of recession in India's major markets—United States and Europe–which turned positive in September 2009, registering a growth of over 160 per cent compared to September 2008, according to EPCH. According to figures available from Directorate General Commercial Intelligence and Statistics (DGCI&S) of the Ministry of Commerce, Exports of handicrafts (other than hand knotted carpets) was merely Rs. 3,870.0 million in 1986-87 when the Export Promotion Council for Handicrafts came into being and from then on it has risen to Rs. 87,189.4 million in year 2009-10.

Item-wise export of handicrafts during 2009-10 over 2008-09 shows art metalware fetching the country Rs. 18,77.64 million in 2009-10 as against 17,902.7 million in the previous year, woodware Rs. 7,173 million against Rs. 6,227.8 million, hand-printed textiles and scarves Rs. 11,733 million against Rs. 11,168.6 million, embroidered and crocheted goods Rs. 31,168.5 million against Rs. 29,369.8 million, shawls as art-ware Rs. 1,31 7.4 million against 1,190.7 million, zari and zari goods Rs. 1,849.1 million against Rs. 1,751.3 million, imitation jewelry Rs. 2,458.3 million against Rs. 2,082.8 million and miscellaneous handicrafts Rs. 12,713.0 million against Rs. 12,139.5 million, according to EPCH figures.

As would be evident from these figures, embroidered and crocheted goods fetched the highest return, followed by art metalware, hand-printed textiles imitation jewelry, zari and zari goods and shawls as artware.

A wide range of handicrafts are produced all over India. Uttar Pradesh and Rajasthan are two states where handicrafts production is concentrated. Moradabad is known for its art metalware production. Jaipur, the capital of Rajasthan, produces almost all items of handicrafts. Besides these two, other major centers for handicrafts production are Agra, Amroha, Aligarh and Saharanpur in UP, Jodhpur, Jaisalmer and Barmer in Rajasthan, Bangalur and Mysore in Karnataka, Chennai in Tamil Nadu, Behrampur and Shantiniketan in West Bengal, Ahmedabad, capital of Gujarat, Kulu, Manali and Dharamshala in Himachal Pradesh, Indore in Madhya Pradesh, Kolhapur in Maharashtra, Srinagar in Jammu and Kashmir and in Kerala.

The export of shawls as artware was of the order of Rs. 1,102.3 million in 2005-06, showing a growth of 105.46 per cent over Rs. 536.5 million in the previous year. In fact, shawls as artware, which fetched a lowly Rs. 178.2 million in 1996-97, jumped suddenly to Rs. 2,040 million in 1999-2000 from Rs. 263.1 million in 1998-99. The item showed further growth to Rs. 2,454 million in 2000-01, but declined to Rs. 944.2 million in 2001-02. Thereafter, there was a slump to Rs. 432.7 million in 2003-04 after a rise of 5.26 per cent in the previous year. The export of shawls as artware was Rs. 1317.4 million in 2009-10. Still, it was far below the level attained in 2000-01.

All other items have shown a steady growth, although there may have been a decline in a particular year or two. Thus, art metal ware has grown to Rs. 18,776 million in 2009-10 from Rs. 17,902.7 million in the previous year. It was again far below Rs. 36,000 million or so attained in 2005-06. Wood ware rose to Rs. 8,530 million in 2005-06 from Rs. 2,187 million in the previous year. Hand printed textiles and scarves rose to Rs. 20,537 million from Rs. 6,861 million, embroidered and crocheted goods to Rs. 47,114.5 million from Rs. 10,308.9 million, zari and zari goods to Rs. 3,470.6 million from Rs. 645.7 million and imitation jewelry to Rs. 2,748 million from Rs. 486.5 million. Overall exports of handicrafts have grown to Rs. 145,268.5 million in 2005-06 from Rs. 38,152.1 million in 1996-97. Exports of handicrafts was a miniscule Rs. 110 million in 1960-61.

United States has been India's largest market for handicrafts, far outstripping United Kingdom and Germany, which were the next two major markets. Except in shawls as artware, in which UAE was the top importer from India in 2009-10, United States outstripped other countries in all other items. In 2009-10, United States imported Rs. 24,891 million worth of handicrafts as against Rs. 22,557.5 in the previous year. Yet, it was far below Rs. 44,627.6 million in 2005-06. United Kingdom imported Rs. 9,280 million worth of handicrafts in 2009-10 against Rs. 16,695.5 million. In 2005-06, import of handicraft by Germany in 2009-10 was Rs. 7,825 million, much below Rs. 15,265.0 million attained by her in 2005-06.

Other major markets were France, which imported Rs. 3,866 million worth of handicrafts in 2009-10, much below Rs. 6,157.6 million in 2005-06, the UAE Rs. 517.99 million against Rs. 3,5253 in 2005-06, Italy Rs. 2,945.8 million against Rs. 4,764.0 million, Japan Rs. 2,016 million against Rs. 4,328.6 million, Canada Rs. 2481.3 million against Rs. 4,502.5 million, the Netherlands Rs. 2,487 million against Rs. 4,166.3 million, Switzerland Rs. 1,212.6 million against Rs. 2,298.9 million and Australia Rs. 1,173 million against Rs. 2,348.4 million.

United States imported in 2009-10, Rs. 24,894 million worth of art metalware, Rs. 1,961.7.846.7 million worth of woodware, Rs. 3,300 million worth of hand printed textiles and scarves, Rs. 9,394.2 million worth of embroidered and crocheted goods, Rs. 502.4 million worth of zari and zari goods and Rs. 795 million worth of imitation jewelry. Regarding shawls as artware, Saudi Arabia imported from India Rs. 441.9 million worth. United States came next, importing only Rs. 1,53.5 million worth.

Belgium, Denmark, Greece, Hong Kong, Israel, Malaysia, Norway, Oman, Portugal, Singapore, South Africa, Switzerland and Sweden were other countries, which imported handicraft items of significant value, according to figures available from DGCI&S. The figures also show that some Latin American countries, like Argentina, Brazil, Chile, Colombia, Equador, Mexico and Venezuela are potential markets. The figures also show that the African continent, which does not have a major buyer besides South Africa, needs to be cultivated.

To promote exports to Africa and Latin America, the Export Promotion Council for Handicrafts organized a Buyer-Seller Meet in South Africa and another in Sao Paulo, Brazil. The response received by the members in South Africa was encouraging and the delegates reported on the spot business and trade enquiries to the tune of US $374,200.00 during the three days of the event. The response received in Sao Paulo was equally encouraging and the delegates reported on the spot business and trade enquiries to the tune of US $ 627,800.00 during the two days of the meet.

Handicrafts is a labour intensive industry with high potential for employment, particularly of the poorer sections of society in rural areas and is spread all over the country. It is economically important in view of low capital investment, high value addition, negligible import content and high potential for export earnings. It, therefore, needs all encouragement from the government, both Central and the States to help the Export Promotion Council for Handicrafts which is making all efforts in the direction.

9

Engineering Goods

(Machine tools, capital goods, consumer goods, machinery and instruments, transport equipment and electronic hardware)

Engineering is a vital sector of the world economy, contributing 30 per cent to world trade. India has registered impressive growths in the sector with export of 40.83 per cent in 2004-05 compared to the previous year. When compared to 2000-01, engineering exports registered a growth of 156.31 per cent in 2004-05. However, exports of goods and services declined in 2009-10 to Rs. 1,599,359 million as against Rs. 1,890,105 million in the previous year. The decline was obviously due to the global recession, as in the case of many other items. Exports of all groups, except "non-ferrous metals and products thereof," registered a decline. Non-ferrous metals, registered a marginal growth of 2.47 per cent.

The extent of growth in exports of items comprising engineering goods could be seen if one goes back to 1960-61. Exports of machinery, transport and metal manufactures, including iron and steel, amounted to a mere US $46 million (Rs. 220 million) in 1960-61, according to the Economic Survey 2005-06. Exports of these items, according to the Survey, went up to US $17,274 million (Rs. 776,130 million) in 2004-05.

Machine tools, or mother machines, comprise an important item under engineering exports. However, such varied and complex are the items under the head of engineering exports that the Engineering Export Promotion Council (EEPC) has set up 39 panels to promote the exports of these items, including one on machine tools.

The term machine tool is usually reserved for tools that use a power source. Machine tools really began to develop after the development of steam engine, leading to the Industrial Revolution. Today, most are powered by electricity.

In engineering exports, EEPC data also includes exports of management and technical services. Exports of these services grew by 17.42 per cent to US $245.32 million in 2004-05 from US $208.92 million in the previous year.

Besides machine tools, engineering exports comprise capital goods, primary iron and steel and items thereof, prime iron and steel, including ferro alloys, iron and steel products (manufactured), non-ferrous metals and products thereof and consumer durables, according to group-wise figures provided by the EEPC. Each group showed good growth during 2004-05 when compared to the previous year, as also to 2000-01.

Machine Tools

India imported machine tools from 35 countries in 2005-06. It exported machine tools to countries double that number during that year. Japan was the biggest exporter to India, other major exporters being Italy, Republic of Korea, United States, UK, Netherlands and Hong Kong.

India's exports of machine tools was far less than its imports, but in the six years since 2001-02, the exports more than doubled. The maximum growth of 28.54 per cent was in 2005-06 as per data available from the Directorate General Commercial Intelligence and Statistics (DGCI&S). In 2008-9, exports jumped to Rs. 17,224.05, but slumped to Rs. 13,343.56 million in 2009-10, according to provisional data reported by DGCI&S.

India-made machine tools are currently exported to over 50 countries, the major ones being the United States, Italy, Germany, SAARC countries and the Middle East. The United States was India's leading market for machine tools, as also for manufactures of metals together worth Rs. 34,858 million.

Other major importers of machine tools in 2004-05 were the UAE, the UK, Germany, Italy, Bangladesh, Nigeria, Singapore, Sri Lanka, Saudi Arabia, China, Canada and Iran, ranging in terms of value from Rs. 640.41 million in the case of the UAE to Rs. 102.80 million in the case of Iran. Countries importing machine tools from India worth less than Rs. 100 million, but more than Rs. 40 million, included France, Indonesia, Kenya, Korea, Malaysia, Sudan and Switzerland.

The Indian machine tool industry needs to do more aggressive marketing. On an average, the industry exports 6 per cent of its sales and the biggest among them, Hindustan Machine Tools, exports 10 per cent. The growth in the industry is demand driven, which is coming from automobile, defence, space and textile machinery industry, all of which are at their peak.

Capital Goods

Exports of capital goods registered a growth of 37.40 per cent to US $4,263.59 million in 2004-05 compared to US $3,102.96 million in the previous year and 176.85 per cent when compared to US $1,540.00 million in 2000-01. In 2009-10, however, capital goods registered a decline of 8.70 per cent to Rs. 761,134.6 million from 833,629 million in the previous year. Capital goods comprise textile and jute mill machinery, knitting machinery, sugar and cement mill machinery, boilers, other chemical plants, including machinery for paper, water treatment, food processing, including pharmaceutical machinery, heating and cooling equipment, cranes, lift and winches, other construction machinery, including earth moving equipment, tractors and agricultural equipment and other industrial machinery.

Capital goods sector also includes electrical power equipment, T.L. towers and parts, fencing structures, freight containers, other structurals, electric wires and cables, wagons and coaches, coastal vessels and ships, aircraft and aerospace equipment, commercial vehicles, including jeeps and cars and two and three wheelers (for details see the heading 'transport equipment'). Exports of all items in capital goods category registered good growth, excepting textile and jute mill machinery, electric wires and cables and aircraft and aerospace equipment, which received declines.

Consumer Goods

In consumer goods category, which includes auto parts, bicycles and parts, hand tools, cutting tools, steel files, I.C. engines and parts, air compressors, mechanical pumps, electric fans and parts, mica and mica products, office equipment, dry batteries, storage batteries, sewing machines and needles, scientific, surgical and other instruments, exports showed a decline of 7.93 per cent in 2009-10, going down to Rs. 266,197 million as against Rs. 289,129 million in the previous year, according to figures available from the Engineering Export Promotion council (EEPC).

Machinery and Instruments

The exports of machinery and instruments surged to Rs. 502,418.57 million in 2008-09 from Rs. 97,199.06 million in 2002-03. However, in the very next year, the exports are estimated to have declined to Rs. 471,930.52 million, according to data available from DGCI&S.

In the case of machinery and instruments, the UAE followed the USA in 2004-05 with imports worth Rs. 11,345.42 million from India. Other major markets for India were the UK, Germany, Singapore, China, Nigeria, Italy, Netherlands, Indonesia, Iran, Sri Lanka, Bangladesh and France.

Australia, Saudi Arabia, Japan, Egypt, Thailand, South Africa, Belgium, Canada, Republic of Korea, Brazil, Nepal, Turkey, Spain, Tanzania, Switzerland and Sudan were among others in the reckoning in 2004-05.

Major Markets

Overall, the USA has been the largest market for engineering goods from India, importing US $2,336.35 million worth in 2004-05, registering a growth of 76.69 per cent over the previous year. The UAE was the second largest market while China emerged as the third largest market, according to EEPC data.

Taken together, Europe provided the largest market with imports of around US $3,500 million in 2004-05. In country-wise imports for the year, the UK is in the lead, importing US $786.68 million worth. It was followed by Italy, Germany, Belgium, Spain, France, the Netherlands, Greece, Denmark, Russia, Switzerland, Sweden, Finland, Ireland, Hungary, Austria and Bulgaria.

SAARC and ASEAN

EEPC figures show that neighbouring SAARC countries too could emerge as good markets with Sri Lanka importing during 2004-05 engineering goods worth US $360.38 million, Bangladesh US $304.45 million and Nepal US $160.37 million. Even a small country like Bhutan imported engineering goods worth US $48.03 million.

ASEAN too was a good emerging market with Singapore importing engineering goods worth US $605.22 million from India in 2004-05, showing a growth of 128.21 per cent over the previous year. In 2005-06, its imports nearly doubled. Indonesia, Malaysia, Philippines, Vietnam, Myanmar, Cambodia, Laos and Brunei were among countries in ASEAN, providing good market for engineering goods from India. Africa too provided good market with India's exports to South Africa, Nigeria, Libya, Kenya and Egypt going up handsomely in 2005-06. In the case of Sudan, however, there was a 24.14 per cent decline.

Some of the other countries in Africa too were emerging as good markets for India. The countries included Ghana, Tanzania, Libya, Morocco, Uganda, Congo Democratic

Republic, Mozambique Senegal, Zambia, Ethiopia, Benin, Cote D'Ivoire, Malawi, Tunisia, Mali, Guinea and Angola, each importing more than Rs. 10 million worth in 2005-06. Only in the case of Burkina Faso, Liberia, Cameroon, Gambia, Chad, Namibia Botswana, Zimbabwe and Somali, imports were less than US $ ten million.

In West Asia, Saudi Arabia, Iran and Oman were major markets, importing engineering goods worth more than US $100 million in 2005-06. Imports by the other countries in 2005-06 too were sizeable. The countries included Qatar, Kuwait, Syria, Bahrain, Iraq, Yemen and Jordon.

Imports of engineering goods from India by Russia and the Commonwealth of Independent States was miniscule and left much to be desired. Imports by Russia was a lowly US $51.58 million in 2004-05, although it showed growth over the previous year. In the case of Kazakhstan, its imports came down to US $11.47 million in 2004-05 from US $13.88 million in the previous year. Imports by Uzbekistan, Azerbaijan, Kyrgyzstan and Tajikistan were less than US $10 million.

India Quality Supplier

India has come to be known as a quality supplier of engineering goods. This is what accounts for good demand from the USA, Europe, ASEAN and West Asia. Demand is growing even in distant Latin American States. India needs to work its way up to be a dominant player in the global market for engineering goods, particularly in machine tools, capital goods and machinery and appliances.

Primary Iron and Steel

Exports of primary iron and steel and ferro alloys showed the maximum growth of 205.44 per cent to US $584.40 million in 2004-05 from US $84.60 million in the previous year. Prime iron and steel, including pig iron had a growth of 56.15 per cent to US $3,781.24 million from US $2,340.72 million in the *previous year. When compared to 2000-01, the growth was 285 per cent from US $981.88 million. Steel pipes and tubes, ferrous hollow-ware, electrodes, bolts, nuts and screws, railway track materials, wire ropes and strands, sanitary castings, industrial castings and forgings, razor blades, steel furniture and other steel products had a growth of 37.84 per cent to US $2,753.76 million in 2004-05 from US $1,997.86 million in the previous year.*

According to DGCI&S data, ferro alloys worth Rs. 12,027.91 million were exported during 2004-05, aluminium other than products, worth Rs. 11,209.96 million, non-ferrous metals worth Rs. 34,369.13 million, manufactures of metal worth Rs. 17,047.75 million, iron and steel, bar and rods worth Rs. 18,035.61 million and primary and semi-finished iron and steel worth Rs. 158,142.80 million, all totalling Rs. 691,182.24 million.

Iron and Steel

There are two item groups in the category of iron and steel- iron and steel, bar and rod, etc and primary and semi-finished iron and steel—for exports. The imports consisted of iron and steel, primary steel and pig iron-based items. India's import of iron and steel exceeded its exports by Rs.45,332.29 million. The total exports were of the order of Rs.157,096.12 million, while imports totalled Rs. 202,428.41 million.

India exported iron and steel , bar and rod, etc. to more than 140 countries, major markets for the country were Italy, importing Rs. 4,951.31 million worth, followed by the USA, Germany, Myanmar. Malaysia, Nigeria, Turkey, Nepal, Netherlands, China, the UAE and Sri Lanka.

India imported primary steel and pig-iron based products of the value of Rs. 8,250.20 million and iron and steel worth Rs. 194,172.21 million. Major countries from which primary steel and pig iron products were imported are China worth Rs. 2,677.18 million followed by Bhutan, Brazil, Columbia Austria and the United Kingdom.

Peoples Republic of Korea was India's largest source of iron and steel, exporting to India Rs. 18,929.48 million worth. Other major countries exporting iron and steel to India were Belgium, the Netherlands, Nepal, Brazil, Malaysia, Austria, Australia, Canada, Belarus, Bhutan and Mexico.

Non-ferrous Metal

Non-ferrous metals and products, which consist of aluminium and aluminium products and other non-ferrous metals and products are also dealt with by the EEPC in primary iron and steel items. Exports of aluminium and aluminium products received a growth of 27.48 per cent to US $517 million in 2004-05 from US $504 million in the previous year, according to EEPC. Exports of non-ferrous metals and products received a growth of 57.10 per cent to US $1,005.70 million in 2004-05 from US $640.17 million in the previous year.

The UAE was India's top market in 2004-05 for non-ferrous metal, importing from India Rs. 5,806.75 million worth. It was followed by Taiwan, Thailand, China, Saudi Arabia, Republic of Korea and Oman, each importing more than Rs. 1,000 million worth.

Ferro Alloys

In ferro alloys, China with imports worth Rs. 3,035.64 million in 2004-05 was the largest market, followed by Japan, Italy, and Republic of Korea. The UAE was India's largest market for non-ferrous metals, importing Rs. 5,806.75 million worth, followed among others by Taiwan, Thailand, Saudi Arabia, Singapore, Republic of Korea, Oman and Sri Lanka.

In residual chemicals again China was the largest market, importing from India Rs. 3,518.41 million worth of the items, followed by the USA, the UK, Japan, the UAE, Saudi Arabia and Singapore.

Aluminium

Singapore was the largest market for aluminium other than products, importing from India Rs. 3,770.23 million worth in 2004-05. Vietnam came next with imports worth Rs. 1,249.69 million. It was followed by Bangladesh. China, the UAE, Iran, Thailand, Indonesia, Sri Lanka, Germany, Malaysia and the USA.

Mica

India exported mica worth Rs. 1361.69 million in 2008-09, nearly double that of Rs. 770.11 million in 2005-06. In 2001-02, exports were a measly Rs. 26.58 million. China was the largest importer of mica in 2005-06 with imports worth Rs. 252.13 million, followed by Japan Rs. 110.69 million, the USA Rs. 93.91 million and the Netherlands Rs. 62.87 million.

Transport Equipment

Transport equipment industry has grown at a staggering pace over the last few years. The opening up of the sector over the last decade has caught the attention of global auto majors as the only market rival to China, in terms of potential market size and growth opportunity. As the automobile industry has grown and matured, the Indian auto components industry has also grown tremendously, and is rapidly achieving global competitiveness both in terms of cost and quality.

The Indian automobile industry has a diverse base comprising 15 manufacturers of cars and multi-utility vehicles, nine of commercial vehicles, 14 of two and three-wheelers, and 10 tractor manufacturers. Apart from these, there are five automobile engine manufacturers and a large auto ancillary sector consisting of over 400 companies in the organized sector and 5,000 in the unorganized sector. Investment in the industry exceeded US $10 billion at the start of the decade and the turnover was approximately US $12.5 billion. Direct employment was estimated at 500,000 and indirect employment at 10 million.

The total installed capacity of four-wheelers in the country in 2005-06 was 1.72 million, for two and three wheelers 9.13 million and for engines 0.18 million. The turnover of the automobile industry has gone up to Rs. 835,851 million in 2005-06 from Rs. 661,769 million in the previous year.

The auto components industry also made rapid progress with production going up from US $2.4 billion in 1995-96 to US $3.6 billion in 2001-02. Production is estimated at US $6.7 billion in 2004-05 and is projected to rise to US $40 billion by 2015. Export of auto components went up to US $400 million by 2001-02 and crossed the US $1 billion mark in 2004-05.

The US $ 6.7 billion industry has registered a cumulative annual growth rate (CAGR) of 17 per cent during 1998-2003 and is projected by the Auto Components Manufacturers Association of India (ACMA) to grow at a 15 per cent CAGR till fiscal 2012. In fact, industry observers are of the view that while the Indian automobile market will grow at a measured pace, the auto components industry is poised for a take-off and is one of the few industries where India has a distinct competitive advantage.

The export of transport equipment, which consists of automobiles and auto ancillaries and components, recorded more than three fold growth in three years, going up to Rs. 202,177 million in 2005-06 from Rs. 64,554.36 million in 2002-03. The exports went up to Rs. 127,141.77 million in 2004-05 and is estimated to have grown to 202,177 million in 2005-06, escalating to Rs. 572,972.90 million in 2008-09. The exports are estimated to have slid to Rs. 471,930.52 million in 2009-10.

With the galloping growth in the sector, exports are expected to do even better in the coming years. Auto magnates are already on the job, promoting and projecting export growth not only during the coming year, but for several years ahead.

The exponential growth in the sector was spurred by the entry of global automobile companies in the mid-nineties with the average growth rate touching 22 per cent. Major automobile companies operating in the country include Maruti Udyog Ltd, having collaboration with Suzuki of Japan, Volvo,

Daimler, Chrysler, Delphi, Toyota, Ford, General Motors and Hyundai. There are around 257 joint ventures with Japanese, German, British, American, French and Korean firms–Japan leading the pack with 74 tie-ups with Indian companies.

With the growth in installed capacity, production too has gone up in different categories. The production of medium and heavy commercial vehicles (M&HCs) has gone up to 219,297 units in 2005-06 from 96,752 units in 2001-02, showing a growth of 126 per cent. The production of light commercial vehicles (LCVs) has gone up to 171,781 units from 65,756 registering a growth of 161 per cent. Similar has been the case with passenger cars, with its production crossing one million for the first time–1,045,881 units to be exact. The production of two wheelers, comprising scooters, motorcycles and mopeds, which has been the largest segment in the automobile industry, went up to 7,600,801 units in 2005-06 from 4,271,327 units in 2001-02.

More than 185 countries imported transport equipment from India in 2004-05, most of them of small value. Major markets for transport equipment for India were the United States with imports worth Rs. 14,574.11 million in 2004-05. The USA was followed by France, Sri Lanka, the UK, Italy, Singapore, Germany, Mexico, Nepal, Columbia, Bangladesh, the Netherlands, Saudi Arabia, Belgium, Nigeria, France and Malaysia each importing more than a Rs. 1,000 million worth, some of them several fold. Egypt too was a major market, falling short of the Rs. 1,000 million by Rs. 33 million.

In the case of Singapore, its imports of transport equipment from India shot up to Rs. 29,228.39 million in 2005-06, according to provisional figures available from DGCI&S. In the case of three other countries, India's exports of transport equipment more than doubled in 2005-06. In the case of Egypt, exports jumped to Rs. 1,967.43 million in 2005-06 from 967.40 million in the previous year. Similarly, in the case of Kuwait, its imports shot up to Rs. 1,299.85 million from Rs. 377.37 million, while in the case of Argentina, it galloped to Rs. 1,217.78 million from Rs. 431.57 million.

The growth of the automobile sector is linked to the growth in the auto components industry. Indian, made component of cars, manufactured in the country, is about 85 per cent, with 15 per cent specialized components still being imported. The auto components industry made rapid progress with production going up from US $2.4 billion in 1995-96 to US $3.6 billion in 2001-02. Production is estimated at US $6.7 billion in 2004-05 and is projected to rise to US $40 billion by 2015. Export of auto components went up to US $400 million by 2001-02 and crossed US $1 billion mark in 2004-05. The largest market for auto ancillaries are the US and the EU, with a market share of 28 per cent each, while Asia and Africa account for 27 per cent and 11 per cent respectively.

The auto-components industry, which has been growing at the rate of 30%, has been exporting around 15 per cent of its output, according to ACMA. In the year 2003-04, the industry exported US $1 billion worth of transport equipment as against US $ 760 million worth in the previous year. Principal export items include replacement parts, tractor parts, motorcycle parts, piston rings, gaskets, engine valves, fuel pump nozzles, fuel injection parts, filter & filter elements, radiators, gears, leaf springs, brake assemblies and bearings, clutch facings, head lamps, auto bulbs and halogen bulbs, spark plugs and body parts. ACMA represents over 479 companies, whose production forms a majority of the total auto component output in the organized sector.

By international standards, the auto parts and ancillary hardware makers in India are small and lack specialized technology for export. Technology, to begin mass production at American and Japanese standards, will have to come through technology transfer. The latter is possible with sharp US focus to make India into a strategic sourcing centre, very much in line with India becoming a strategic sourcing centre for software development. The latter took seven years. India could be a major supplier of auto parts earlier than that. Exports of different group categories in terms of numbers, according to figures available from Society of Indian

Automobile Manufacturers (SIAM), show equally good growth. As per these figure 170,193 passenger cars were exported in 2005-06 as against 49,273 in 2001-02 showing a growth of 245 per cent. Export growth in utility vehicles went up by 192 per cent to 14,096 from 4,824 in 2001-02 and that of LCVs to 26,485 from 7,046 during the same period, showing a growth of 275 per cent. In multi-purpose utility vehicles, exports have gone up by 43.34 per cent to 5,579 units with from 3802 units.

In commercial vehicles (medium and heavy category), 14,096 units were exported in 2005-06, showing a growth of 192 per cent over 4,824 in 2001-02. In LCV category, 26,485 units were exported as against 7,046 in 2001-02, showing a growth of 275 per cent. In three wheelers category, there was a growth in exports of 397 per cent to 76,885 units as against 15,462 in 2001-02.

In two wheelers, 83,873 scooters and 396,202 motorcycles were exported showing a growth of 196 per cent and 579 per cent over 28,332 and 56,880 units respectively in the years under reference. Motor cycles, thus, showed the maximum growth in exports during the period. Mopeds showed a growth of 127.61 per cent with exports of 43,181 units as against 18,971 units.

A window of opportunity has opened up to scores of component manufacturers, who are bagging huge export orders from global auto majors. Rico Auto, manufacturers of components, recently bagged orders worth Rs. 590 million from Ford's UK operations for two components the company makes. It also picked up orders for components that were to be fitted in Land Rover and Jaguar. Bharat Forge has acquired a Rs. 600 million order to supply forgings to a heavy commercial manufacturer in China. All MNC car majors are planning to source components from India and Indian component manufacturers are ready to grab that opportunity.

The success with indigenously designed products–Scorpio of Mahindra, Pulsar of Bajaj and Tata Indica, TVS Victor and LML's Freedom – has lent a lot of good to industry confidence.

The transport equipment market is set for further growth with Piaggio returns to the country and Tatas launching Nano, its Rs. 1 lakh (Rs. 100,000) car. Tata Motors plan to sell one million of its Rs. 1 lakh cars, although it says with inflation pushing up costs of components, it may not be possible to stick to Rs. 1 lakh value of the car.

The country's commercial vehicles sector has grown exponentially over the last two three years and a host of global players, including Scania, MAN, Valvo and domestic companies, such as Tata Motors, Ashok Leyland are stepping into make the most of the boom in the sector. Having withstood foreign competition in India, and in the process of doing so abroad, Indian industry is close to international quality norms.

Thanks to cheap availability of labour, engineering skills and a new thrust on quality and cost reduction, Indian auto companies are today highly competitive in the global market. Most of the car manufacturers are looking at establishing their presence in the international market to improve their volumes, thereby realizing economies of scale by leveraging on foreign markets. Exports of transport equipment, thus, have a good future as it is one of the fast growing sectors in the global market.

Electronic Hardware

India's excellence in computer software is known the world over. Now electronic hardware too is emerging as a major player in the country, although its exports are still a fraction of software in value terms.

Total electronics hardware (electronic goods and computer Software in physical form) exports in 2008-09 was Rs. 328,579.61 million compared to around Rs. 80,000 million in 2004-05. Exports in 2004-05 were a little more than 10 per cent of Rs. 773,000 million worth of software exports, which also included Information Technology Enabled Services (ITES), according to figures available from DGCI&S and the Electronics and Computer Software Export Promotion Council (ESC). Nevertheless, in CDRs and DVDs, the country has global capacity and is already meeting 20 per cent of world requirements, as per industry claims.

India's exports of electronic goods, which comprise computer hardware, electronic components, instruments – office equipment and medical equipment – and telecom equipment, have gone up to its level of Rs. 80,000 million in 2004-05 from Rs. 77,000 million in 2003-04, registering a 3.9 per cent growth. The growth in 2003-04 was 37.5 per cent over Rs. 56,000 million in 2002-03, as per ESC figures.

India is poised to be a leading player in electronics hardware exports by being a part of the global electronics network. The need is to blend our competence in software with hardware, says ESC. What is more significant is that the solid growth in the export of electronics hardware was mainly triggered by computer hardware. Export in this segment during 2003-04 has grown by 162 per cent. In value terms, the export of computer hardware went up to Rs. 14,400 million in the year compared to Rs. 5,500 million in the previous year. There was, however, a 16.67 per cent decline in 2004-05.

Exports of electronic components have also shown an average growth of 25.92 per cent during the period 1999-2000 to 2004-05. The growth was a healthy 56.46 per cent in 2003-04 over the previous year. In value terms, exports have grown from Rs. 24,000 million in 2002-03 to Rs. 37,550 million in 2003-04. The growth in 2004-05 was a meager 1.19 per cent to Rs. 38,000 million as against Rs. 37,550 million in the previous year.

Exports of electronic instruments, office equipment and medical equipment (OE/ME), have shown a decline of 0.99 per cent in 2004-05 in rupee terms from Rs. 15,150 million to Rs. 15,000 million. Moreover, the average annual growth of OE/ME during the period 1999-2000 to 2004-05 has been 54.57 per cent. Exports of consumer electronics have shown a good growth of 39.39 per cent in 2004-05, going up to Rs. 11,500 million from Rs. 8,250 million. Exports of telecom equipment and cables have shown a hefty growth of 112.12 per cent to Rs. 350 million from Rs. 165 million. However, exports of the item registered a steep decline of 67 per cent in 2003-04 as compared to the previous year. The average annual growth in electronic hardware as a whole was 25.20 per cent.

India's major destinations for electronic hardware exports in 2004-05 were the USA (Rs. 19,112 million), followed by Sweden, Singapore, Germany, Hong Kong, United Kingdom, the UAE, Turkey, Malaysia, the Netherlands, Japan, Belgium, Australia and Canada.

Uninterrupted Power Supply (UPS) was the largest among electronics instrumentation exported from India. Major markets for UPS with exports from India worth Rs. 5,770.09 million in 2004-05 were the USA, the Netherlands, Ireland and Singapore. Medical instruments and appliances, amounting to Rs. 3,225.88 million went among others to the USA, Singapore, Germany, Hong Kong, the Netherlands, the UK, Malaysia and the UAE. Meters worth Rs. 506.38 million were imported from India among others by Malaysia, the UK, New Zealand, Iraq, Spain, Singapore, the USA and the UAE.

Electric Inverters worth Rs. 390.08 million went to Netherlands, Germany, Australia, the UAE, Nepal, Malawi and Nigeria among others. Solar Lights and lamps worth Rs. 382.62 million found a ready market in Germany, which imported 94.35 per cent of India's total exports of the item. The rest were imported by South Africa, Uganda and Philippines. Process control equipment worth Rs. 242.95 million was imported among others by the UK, which lapped up 73.72 per cent of India's total exports of the item. Others included China, Japan, the USA, Singapore and Australia. Electronics Assemblies and Sub-Assemblies valued at Rs. 146.23 million went to Germany, Columbia, the U.K., China, the USA, Philippines, Malaysia and France. Automated Teller Machines (ATM) worth Rs. 160 million were sold to the USA, Canada, Australia, Belgium, Germany and the Netherlands.

Despite a fall in the production of telecommunications equipment, exports registered a high growth of 112 per cent during 2004-05 over the previous year. In telecom equipment, the export of miscellaneous transmission apparatus registered a massive growth of 651 per cent to Rs. 840 million in 2004-05 from Rs. 111.8 million in the previous year. Export of telephone sets also received a high growth of 145 per cent in 2004-05 to Rs. 507.8 million from Rs. 113.1 million. Exports of optical fiber cable, miscellaneous telecom equipment, satellite telecommunication equipment registered growth during 2004-05, while export of switching equipment and EPBAX registered a decline.

Singapore, Hong Kong and other South Asian countries have emerged as India's top destination in the export of telecom equipment during 2004-05. Export of telecom equipment to this region registered a growth of 618 per cent to Rs. 2,440 million during 2004-05 from Rs. 340 million in the previous year. Exports to African countries went up to Rs. 427 million in 2004-05 from Rs. 244.5 million in the previous year with Africa emerging as the second top destination for India's telecom equipment. Exports to the EU, the Far East and Oceanic countries registered growth in exports during 2004-05, while North America and West Asia registered decline.

Major items in consumer electronics are colour TVs, PA systems, clocks and watches, video projectors and parts, electronics flash lights and discharge lamps, black and white TVs, radio communication receivers (audio), recorded CD audio, recorded audio cassettes and digital versatile disc player (DVD). Colour TV remains the top item during the year 2004-05 with exports worth Rs. 4,186.84 million. Export of PA systems increased from Rs. 1,151.00 million to Rs. 1,228.02 million in 2004-05. The other major items, which registered growth in export during 2004-05 are electronic flash lights/discharge lamp, radio receivers, recorded CDs, cassettes and DVD players.

Exports of clocks and watches registered a decline of 34 per cent during 2004-05 over the previous year. With the growth in the export of colour TV, export of B&W television sets, no doubt registered a drastic fall to Rs. 93.6 million from Rs. 351.48 million.

West Asian countries remain the top destination for India's consumer electronics exports since the year 2000-2001. Before that Singapore, Hong Kong and other South-east Asian countries, were the top destinations and now stand second. Exports to West Asian countries increased to Rs. 4,019 million in 2004-05 from Rs. 2,468.4 million in the previous year. Exports to Singapore, Hong Kong and other South Asian countries increased by 146.31 per cent to Rs. 3,400 million in 2004-05 from 1,380.4 million in the previous year. Export to EU countries, African countries, Russia and CIS countries also registered growth during 2004-05. Export to North America, non-EU European countries and Latin America registered decline in 2004-05.

The government has announced certain measures to boost electronic hardware industry. Through one of them, supplies of all 217 ITA-1 items from EHTP (Electronic Hardware Technology Parks) units to DTA (Domestic Tariff Area) would now qualify for fulfillment of Net Foreign Exchange Positive (NFEP) criteria. Further, to promote growth in exports of embedded software, hardware is admissible for duty-free import for testing and development purposes. Hardware up to a value of US $10,000 is allowed to be disposed off subject to STPI (Software Technology Parks of India) certification. In addition 100 per cent depreciation is available over a period of three years to computer and computer peripherals for units in EOU/EHTP/STPI and SEZ.

India has all the requisites to help it emerge as a world leader in electronics. 'We have a very good design base, talented engineers and man-power.' However, the country's biggest problem is the inverted duty structure. Finished products are coming at a much lower rate than components.

Some of the measures in the Union Budget for 2004-05 "would render domestic production unviable due to imminent competition for foreign suppliers," according to ESC. One of them, i.e. abolition of excise duty on PCs, would make imports cheaper since no countervailing duty can be imposed on imported item. Moreover, the Budget does not contain any positive measures for augmenting IT exports from the country.

Measures need to be taken to boost production and exports of electronic hardware from the country to make it a global player. China, India's main competitor, produced 50 million television sets, while India produced only two million. Malaysia invited Intel to set up a plant for chips and integrated circuits in Malaysia, Sony has closed down an electronic goods plant in India to enhance production in its plant in Thailand, from where it could import into the country cheaper. After the Free Trade Agreement with Thailand, it was no longer economic to produce electronic goods in the country. India would have to consider measures to support the electronics goods industry, including SMEs to make the country a world leader in hardware, as it is in the field of software.

10

Textiles, RMG : Jute and Coir

(Textiles & RMG of all fibers, raw cotton, including waste, cotton yarn, fabrics and made-ups, natural silk yarn, fabrics and made up, man-made yarn, fabrics and made ups, woolen yarn, fabrics and made ups, handloom, carpets and jute and coir products)

Textiles cover a wide range of fibres, fabrics, made-ups, garments and products, of which readymade garments (RMG) are the most lucrative. The fibres cover cotton, wool, silk, synthetic fibres, jute, coir and products. The products, besides RMG, include such items as toys, decorative slippers (juti) and carpets of jute and coir, wool and silk. The products, mainly of cotton, cover both handloom and mill-made.

The phasing out of Multi-fiber Agreement (MFA) from January 2005 has opened a window of opportunity for the textile industry, particularly manufacturers of (RMG), who have made a serious attempt to exploit it. Indian textile industry has for long been mired in debt and been struggling with over-capacity. But as the deadline for phasing out of MFA drew nearer, the companies began embarking upon expansion and modernization of facilities and debt restructuring as part of preparation for quota-free regime. Nevertheless, India faced stiff competition from China, driven by a sharp fall in the prices of its products.

India exports ready-made garments (RMG) of cotton, including accessories and of all other fibres. Besides RMG, India has been exporting raw cotton including waste, cotton yarn, fabrics and made-ups, man-made staple fibre, natural silk yarn, fabrics and made-up, man-made yarn, fabrics and made-up and woolen yarn, fabrics and made-ups. India is also exporting jute fibre and jute products, as also manufactures of coir, which have a good demand, and carpets of jute and coir, wool and silk.

India also imported textile material, including readymade garments woven and knit, together valued at Rs. 141,690.15 million in 2008-09. Besides RMG, India imported woolen yarn and fabric, cotton yarn and fabric, manmade filament/spun yarn, made-up textile articles, other textile yarn, fabric and made up articles, jute raw, silk raw, wool raw, synthetic and regenerated fibers, silk yarn and fabrics, woolen and cotton rags and cotton raw, combed/uncombed and waste.

RMG

In textiles, ready-made garments have gained particularly as in the Agreement on Textile and Clothing (ATC), the developed countries had kept the removal of quotas on garments to the final phase. It is, thus, from January 2005 that the markets for RMG have opened up completely. India and China are the two preferred sources for textiles and garments, according to a study by US International Trade Commission. India has a strong position in Cotton, while China leads in synthetics.

India exports ready-made garments (RMG) of cotton, including accessories of silk, of man-made fibres, of wool and of other textile material. Of these, RMG of cotton is the preferred lot, far exceeding the export of RMG of other fabrics taken together, e.g. in 2005-06, it was more than three times that of the others. Taken along with raw cotton, including waste, man-made staple fibre, cotton yarn, natural silk, man-made yarn, woolen yarn, fabrics and made-up, India's textile exports add up to Rs. 698,256.73 million in 2005-06.

Exports of RMG during 2008-09 registered a growth of 29.4 per cent to Rs. 381,537.32 million from Rs. 294,812 million in 2005-06. This was significant considering that the growth in 2004-05 over 2003-04, when the exports stood at Rs. 286,879.56 million, was barely 2.76 per cent. The year 2003-04 showed a growth of 7.81 per cent over Rs. 277,713.84 million in the previous year.

While DGCI&S provides details of RMG, according to the fiber used, i.e. cotton, man-made fiber, silk, wool and other fibers, Apparel Export Promotion Council (AEPC) has split the RMG sector into two-1) articles of apparel and clothing accessories knitted and crocheted and 2) articles of apparel and clothing accessories, not knitted or crocheted. As per AEPC data exports of articles of apparel knitted and crocheted fetched the country Rs.118,676.99 million in 2004-05, while articles not knitted and crocheted Rs.176,701.02 million in the same year. The total export of RMG in 2004-05, thus, worked out to Rs.295,378.01 million as per AEPC figures.

Ready-made garments are the most lucrative segment in the textile sector. As per DGCI&S figures, exports of RMG of cotton and accessories was of the value of Rs. 385,227.2 million in 2008-09, showing a growth of 31.81 per cent over Rs. 381,537.32 million in 2005-06. There was, however, a marginal decline in 2009-10, with exports valued at Rs. 507,563.37 million, according to provisional figures available from DGCI&S.

Exports of RMG of cotton from India showed a high growth of 32.76 per cent in 2008-09 to Rs. 385,227.24 million from Rs. 290,154.84 million in 2005-06. In 2005-06, exports presented a poor showing going up merely by 3.24 per cent to Rs. 281,044.45 million from Rs. 226,630.87 million in the previous year. Further, exports in 2001-02 were valued at Rs. 176,460.79 million showing that exports had more than doubled over a decade, according to figures available from the DGCI&S.

Although RMG of silk showed a much higher growth in value terms, it was much below RMG of other fabrics, fetching in 2008-09 Rs. 13,377.35 million, up 15.89 per cent over Rs. 11,543.1 million in 2005-06, compared to Rs. 8,516.46 million in the previous year. Exports of RMG of wool showed a rise of 5.15 per cent to Rs. 16409.31 million in 2005-06 over Rs.15,605 million in the previous year. The export of RMG of man-made fibres did much better in 2008-09, going up to Rs. 47,219.35 million from Rs. 45,422.11 million in 2005-06. The growth was a high of 36.76 per cent in 2005-06 over Rs. 33,212.26 million in the previous year. Exports of RMG of other textile material, did still better, going up by 114 per cent to Rs. 38,681.13 million in 2008-09 over Rs. 18,007.96 million in 2005-06. In 2005-06, itself, the growth was a high of 66 per cent over Rs.10,847.56 million in the previous year.

RMG of Cotton

Cotton garments were being exported to more than 195 countries. The United States, has been the single largest market for cotton garments from India. It imported in 2005-06 cotton garments worth Rs. 123,176.42 million. The United States was followed by the UK, which imported cotton garments worth Rs. 37,046 million.

Other major markets in 2005-06 were Germany, France, Denmark, the UAE, Italy, Canada, Netherlands, Saudi Arabia and Spain. Russia, another major market, imported from India cotton garments worth only Rs. 1751 million as against Rs. 3,555.29 million in the previous year. Cotton garments of sizable value were also imported from India by Switzerland, Japan, Belgium, Ireland, South Africa, Mexico, Sweden, Norway, Kuwait, Singapore, Turkey and Greece.

Silk

Silk garments have been going to around 134 countries, but of much lower value. The largest market again was the United States, importing silk garments worth Rs. 2,299.28 million in 2004-05. The UK again was the second largest market, importing Rs. 1,026.50 million worth of silk garments in 2004-05. It was followed by the UAE, France, Saudi Arabia, and Germany. Hong Kong, which was not a market for garments of other fibres, imported silk garments worth Rs. 25.82 million.

Synthetic Fibres

RMG of synthetic fibres, where China dominates, went to 168 countries from India in 2004-05, with the United States again having the dominant share, importing from India Rs. 10,132.06 million worth of garments. It was followed by the UAE, the UK, France, Saudi Arabia, Germany, Spain, Italy, Belgium and Canada. Other markets for Indian garments of man-made fibre in 2004-05 were the Netherlands, Sweden, Japan, Malaysia and Mexico.

Wool

In RMG of wool too, United States was the largest market, importing from India Rs. 5,521.76 million worth during 2004-05. The UAE with imports worth Rs. 2,028.96 million was the second largest market, followed by United Kingdom, France, Germany, Saudi Arabia and Russia. Other major markets were Italy, Canada, Spain, Kyrgyzstan, Netherlands, Malaysia, Oman, Japan, Sri Lanka and Belgium.

Other Fibres

Ready-made garments of other textile material went to 165 countries from India in 2004-05 and the USA with imports worth Rs. 2,648.99 million was again on top. UAE, with imports worth Rs. 1,891 million, occupied the second slot, followed by United Kingdom, France, Italy, Saudi Arabia, Canada, Russia, Spain, and Netherlands.

Among neighbours, Sri Lanka imported RMG of other textile material worth Rs. 112.14 million, while Bangladesh worth Rs. 152.67 million in 2004-05.

Other countries, which imported RMG of other textile material in 2004-05 were Belgium, Japan, Malaysia, and Mexico.

Overall, in 2004-05, several countries showed a decline in their import of even RMG of cotton, but for which the growth would have been much higher. Russia was one country, which showed overall decline in RMG of all fibres. With the lifting of the quota system, India would have to make renewed efforts to boost exports to traditional markets.

Other Textile Material

India exported during 2008-09 raw cotton, including waste, worth Rs. 28,658.55 million, a decline from the 2005-06 level when exports stood at Rs. 29,043.54 million. In 2005-06, however, there was a a whopping growth of 587 per cent over Rs. 4,225.78 million in the previous year. India exported in 2008-09 cotton yarn, fabrics and made-ups worth Rs. 189,295.44 million, a growth of 8.38 per cent over Rs. 174,649.21 million in 2005-06, man-made staple fibre worth Rs. 139,187.47 in 2008-09, a growth of 60.57 million over Rs. 86,679 million in 2005-06, natural silk yarn, fabrics and made-up worth Rs. 16,648.22 million, a decline from Rs. 18,951.72 million in 2005-06, man-made yarn, fabrics and made up worth Rs. 139,187 million (Rs. 86,679.45 million) and woolen yarn, fabrics and made-up worth Rs. 4,565.25 million (Rs. 3,775.90 million).

The extent of growth in the market over decades could be realized when one sees that in 1960-61, India exported cotton yarn fabrics and made ups worth only Rs. 650 million, jute manufactures, including twist and yarn worth Rs. 1,350 million and coir yarn and manufactures worth Rs. 60 million.

Indonesia imported from India during 2005-06 cotton raw, including waste worth Rs. 1,211.12 million, while Pakistan imported the item worth Rs. 2007.25 million.

All out effort needs to be made by the industry to promote growth in production and to bring down costs to be able to compete with rivals like China, if the country has to take full advantage of the lifting of the quota system under the Multi-

fibre Agreement. There is evidence that the industry is alive to the challenge. This is amply clear from reports that although average prices are expected to drop by about 10-20 per cent, the exporters are pegging their hopes on offsetting this decline by increasing their volume of sales.

Handloom

The handloom industry, promoted by the Handloom Export Promotion Council (HEPC), has been a testimony to India's rich and varied heritage. Over the years, this industry has stood the test of time and today it proudly commands an enviable position in the world market.

The handloom industry mainly exports fabrics, bed linen, table linen, toilet and kitchen linen, towels, curtains, cushions and pads, tapestries and upholstery, carpets and floor coverings, etc.

The export of handloom products during 2002-03, the year up to which data is available was Rs. 26,332.7 million. The major items fetching good returns include bedcovers and bedspreads (Rs. 2,000.7 million), carpets and floor coverings (Rs. 3,197.5 million) and curtains (Rs. 654.3 million). Among fabrics were lungies *(Rs. 400.6 million),* dhotis *(Rs. 573.8 million),* sarees *(Rs. 163.4 million), shirtings (Rs. 430.7 million) and furnishings (Rs. 142.8 million).*

The USA had 33 per cent share in India's export of handloom products of Rs. 26,332.1 million in 2002-03, while the UK had a share of 9 per cent. Japan and Italy had shares of 4 per cent each, France had a share of 3 per cent, while Canada, Australia and Sweden each had a share of 2 per cent.

In recent years, the handloom industry has adopted various measures and techniques to provide high quality and eco-friendly products to the world market. The manufacturers in India are well aware of AZO free colours and dyes and have discarded the usage of banned materials in the dyeing process with safe substitutes, to ensure eco-friendliness.

The Indian home textile industry has access to excellent infrastructure facilities and uses the latest technology and machinery. Most of the manufacturers have set up 'state of art' modern processing houses to roll out large volumes of high quality products to meet the demands and expectations of the international market. Handloom Export Promotion Council is gearing up its council members for implementing ISO 9000/9002 and ISO 14000 to ensure world class quality and standard.

Western Europe and USA are the major buyers of bed linen from India. The bed sheets are sold either single or in sets with matching pillow cases. Other bed linen varieties, viz. duvet/quilt covers, printed or otherwise decorated are also popular in the international markets. Panipat, Karur and Cannanore are some of the important production centers of this product.

Table linen consists of table cloths, napkins, etc. They are classified as four major varieties namely, flat, plain, checks and woven. The specialty of this product is to come out with a range of flat woven with individual printed designs, jacquards with or without embroidery at the fringes, or plain weaves with more or less embroidery and machine or hand lace items. Karur, Chennimalai, Cannanore, Ghaziabad, Panipat, Delhi and Agra are the main manufacturing centers for Table Linen.

Floor coverings have been made from textile fibres for more than five thousand years. India produces a wide range of handloom cotton floor coverings such as 'galichas', 'durries', druggets, prayer rugs, hooked rugs, 'gabbas' and 'namdas'. Among these hand-woven articles, the durrie (floor spreads) is the most common and is used not only as an ordinary floor covering, but also for ceremonial occasions such as feasts and prayers. The rapid growth and progress of the floor covering industry in recent years has resulted in a large range of complex geometrical, floral, figurative patterns as well as traditional designs, combined with ethnic motifs.

With demands from the United States in recent years, durrie weaving has become a major industry in India. Ninety per cent of the durries available in European and American markets are woven in India. The states of Haryana and Punjab are noted for their production of picturesque cotton durries. Durrie weaving is still a sizable cottage industry in the handloom centers in Haryana, Ludhiana, Amritsar, Jalandhar and Pathankot. Other centers for durrie weaving are Bhavani in Tamil Nadu, Amroha, Agra, Farrukhabad and Hathras in Uttar Pradesh, Bikaner in Rajasthan, Eluru, Adoni, Warrangal and Kurnool in Andhra Pradesh and Jagdalpur in Madhya Pradesh.

Carpet weaving on handlooms came into vogue during the last decade and is gaining popularity since the product is attractive and comparatively cheap. Unlike hand knotted and tufted carpets, the productivity of carpets on handlooms is high.

India is one of the major suppliers of towels to the world market. Towels of various sizes are manufactured here. Bath towels, beach towels, tea towels are made by the terry towel industry to cater to the needs of the ultimate users. Terry fabric is now being used by the industry for creating a range of bath robes for cool and comfortable use.

With a large population of ethnic Indians, Singapore, Malaysia and West Asian countries are the main target markets for 'dhoti', 'lungi' and sari. Dhoti is basically a loin cloth, which is one of the more popular forms of apparel of the Indian male. It is also one of the most ancient recorded Indian drape. The lightweight cotton fabric, also called dhoti, that is used as garment is often usually white and sometimes bordered in colourful stripes. Saudi Arabia, Abu Dhabi, Dubai, Bahrain and Muscat are the potential and growing market for lungis.

'Sari,' a garment of Asian women that consists of several yards of lightweight cloth draped so that one end forms a skirt and the other a head or shoulder covering, has enhanced the beauty of Indian women for ages.

The characteristic item of fabric produced and exported from the Madras and Andhra belt is the Real Madras Handkerchief (RMHK). RMHK is exported chiefly to West African countries such as Benin, Nigeria, Ghana, Sierra Leone, Gambia and Liberia from where it finds its way to surrounding countries such as Southern and Northern Cameroon, Dahomey, Ivory Coast, Guinea, Senegal and to many other places in Central Africa.

In the recent past, these fabrics have made an entry into the market in Western Europe and the USA with slight modifications in the dimensions and constructional particulars of the original product. Several countries have imitated this fabric on power looms and have been attempting to market it. These are known as 'Imitation Madras', while the genuine product from India made on handlooms, came to acquire the prefix 'REAL.'

HEPC along with its Council members, has brought out new range of Indian Textiles where traditional Indian items are thoughtfully converted to world class home textiles. One such product is Comfy Bedroom slippers, designed and constructed to provide total comfort to the wearer. The Comfy range of indoor slippers is aesthetically designed in varied colours and materials. These light weight slippers enable the wearer to shuffle across the room effortlessly.

Another unique product is an aesthetically designed handbag with a blend of leather and cotton textile fabric. This has been the result of a joint initiative of the Handloom Export Promotion Council (HEPC) and the Central Leather Research Institute (CLRI). Being light in weight, with an appealing look, a range of bags has been designed specially for comfort.

The Government is extending financial assistance to exporters for export promotion activities abroad, such as participation in trade delegations, trade fairs and exhibitions. Exporting companies with an f.o.b. value of exports of up to Rs. 150 million in the preceding year are eligible for Market

Development Assistance (MDA) for participation in trade delegations, fairs and exhibitions abroad to explore new markets for export of their specific product(s) and commodities from India.

The handloom industry promoted by the Handloom Export Promotion Council has been a wonderful testimony to India's rich and varied heritage. Over the years, this industry has stood the test of time and today it proudly commands an enviable position in the world market. A new facet of the handloom section has taken shape in the form of home furnishings - the art of weaving has extended beyond saris and has entered home portals - through curtains, table mats, bed linen and so on. It is rather sad that despite the efforts of HEPC, handloom does not figure among commodities, listed by DGCI&S in its monthly bulletins. Further, it has been given Harmonised System Code (H.S. Code) only up to 2002-2003, the year up to which data is available.

Carpets

A legacy of the Mughals, Indian carpets are renowned the world over for exquisite designs, subtle elegance, attractive colours and workmanship. The magnificence of Indian carpet weaving and the intricate patterns that emerged have substantially increased India's carpet exports and placed it prominently in the international carpet market.

Carpet weaving was brought to India by the great Mughal Emperor Akbar in the 16th century. Some of the most exclusive carpets were created during the Mughal reign, each carpet unlike the other, but infused with a common magic of colours and design.

The carpet industry is one industry in India that is almost wholly export-oriented. The cottage industry earns foreign exchange to the tune of Rs. 24,000 million per annum. However, although India ranks number one in terms of numbers, it occupies third place in terms of value share, after Iran and China. India faces stiff competition from these two countries—China with respect to both quality and price and Iran as regards quality of the carpets. The exports of carpets, including silk, was Rs. 36,303.75 million in 2008-89, a decline of 3,97 per cent over Rs. 37,775.54 million in 2005-06. Exports in 2005-06 was of the value of Rs. 28,595.82 million, 30 per cent more than what it was in the previous year.

India is the leading supplier of carpets to the vast American market and has the distinction of being the second largest exporter of carpets globally. Carpets from Bhadohi and Mirzapur are famous worldwide. Initially, Indian carpets were considered poor manifestations of Persian rugs and carpets. Gradually and steadily, they have been accepted as original works of art. They have been accepted in the international markets and come under the good carpets category. The trends in export growth are clear indicators of the change. For a time, involvement of child labour caused a setback to the industry, its growth and exports. It was covered up soon with the hard work of the producers and inputs both from the government and the manufacturers.

Uttar Pradesh tops all carpet exporting states across India and major carpet manufacturers are in cities like Varanasi, Bhadohi, Mirzapur, Agra, Ghosi and Shahjahanpur. Bhadohi and Mirzapur manufacture highest number of carpets with unique look and unmatched style, representing tradition and culture.

The categories of carpets exported by India are handmade woolen carpets, rugs, druggets, 'durries', etc, including cotton carpets, hand-made woolen tufted carpets, hand-made silk carpets and hand-made staple synthetic carpets. Each one of these categories of carpets registered growth both in dollar and rupee terms in 2005-06.

Major importers of Indian carpets are the USA, Britain, Germany, Canada, and Argentina, to which carpet exports have declined. Exports of Indian carpets (including silk carpets) have gone up to Rs. 37,745.49 million in 2005-06 from Rs. 28,595.82 million in 2004-05. However, exports of carpets declined in 2008-09 to Rs. 36,303.75 million, according to figures available from DGCI&S.

The exports of carpets have gone up to this level from Rs. 9,920 million in 1993-94, according to Carpet Export Promotion Council (CEPC). Items included by CEPC in carpets include hand-made woolen carpets, rugs, druggets, durries, including cotton carpets, hand-made silk carpets and hand-made staple/synthetic carpets.

*Exports by India of hand-made woolen carpets, rugs, druggets, '**durries**', including cotton carpets were the largest in value terms, aggregating to Rs. 16,406.5 million in 2005-06. Hand-made woolen tufted carpets came next with exports worth Rs. 8,714.46 million. Exports of hand-made silk carpets were worth Rs. 1,817.00 million, while that of hand-made staple synthetic carpets a meager Rs. 550.5 million. The exports of all categories taken together showed growth during 2005-06 over the previous year.*

The USA was the biggest market for Indian carpets, importing from India Rs. 16,207.66 million worth in 2005-06 as against Rs. 13,682.8 million worth in 2004-05, constituting over 44 per cent of India's exports of carpets. Germany was the second largest market, importing from India Rs. 6,683.70 million worth. Next came United Kingdom with imports worth Rs. 2277.35 million, followed among others by Japan, France, Canada, Switzerland, Australia, Italy, Spain, Belgium, Denmark, The Netherlands, Sweden, Finland, Argentina and Norway.

The recent export order from Swedish retail giant IKEA has given an added fillip to the carpet industry. IKEA, which has a presence in 32 countries worldwide, had indicated that it will be buying carpets for its retail chain from India. The demand, for about four and a half million pieces, is massive. The multinational also plans to buy printed quilt covers from India. With all this, the exports to Sweden are expected to increase by 30% a year for the next few years. On bagging this order, India has been placed eighth among 55 supplier countries. IKEA is known for the social audit it conducts with its refusal to source products from countries that indulge in child and bonded labour. This will reflect favourably on India, especially since there was a taint of flouting child labour law against it in earlier years.

Lately, the demand for hand knotted carpets has been declining across the world, the trend leaning slowly towards other handmade floor coverings like rugs, 'durries', coir mats, hand woven carpets, hand tufted rugs and durries, jute mats and coverings, hand knotted cotton and wool rugs, hand-woven carpets, chain stitch rugs, ikat mattresses, jacquard rugs, etc. Despite this trend, India has managed to retain its position in terms of export value.

Trends in design of carpets are fast becoming an addition to the list of things that are affected by fashion fluctuation. It is increasingly seen that they are as subject to fads and fashions as any sartorial accessory or home décor item. In colour choices, muted beiges and light natural tones, although still popular, are gradually being replaced by bright, vibrant colors. People are ready to have the same colours on their carpets and floor coverings as they have on the rest of their home textiles. Thus pinks, reds, bronzes, rusts, etc. are becoming quite popular. Also gaining popularity is a touch of metallic colours, like gold, silver, or bronze being woven into the pattern for a rich and sumptuous look.

Even more than looks, comfort seems to be of prime consideration now. So carpets with a softer and more luxurious feel are the present rage. Carpet manufacturers are also trying out different yarns in the manufacture of the carpets. Other than the traditional and highly appreciated wool and silk, softer yarns are now in the market.

Carpet industry not only earns the much needed foreign exchange for the country, but provides gainful employment to artisans in rural areas. It provides employment to as many as 250,000 carpet weavers, mostly belonging to weaker sections from rural and backward areas. However, considering the stiff challenges faced by the country in the global market, the Indian Institute of Carpet Technology has been set up at Bhadohi to provide the much needed support to the carpet and floor covering industry in the country.

Carpets have always been a revenue earner for India. From the beginning of this millennium, the industry seems to have been riding a successful wave. If the small exporter is given a little more assistance in terms of infrastructure and export benefits, the industry will do even better. Indian carpet industry follows very old Persian traditional designs and lacks unique identity in the world market. With the opening of the economy and post WTO regime, the carpet industry will have to pay greater attention towards brand building, improving quality and productivity to enhance its share in the global market.

Jute and Coir

Jute fiber is now gaining added importance. Known for gunny bags and packaging material, jute is now being transformed into a glamorous fabric of high fashion. It is a major industry in India, particularly in West Bengal, which has 61 of the total 78 jute mills in the country, together producing 9,500 bales and providing employment to over 273,000 workers. Jute is being cultivated in India for centuries. Jute industry in India dates back to 1854 when the first jute mill was set up by George Auckland at Rishra in Hoogly district of West Bengal.

Currently the production of the fiber in India is around 10 million bales and about 78 jute mills are operating in the country at present. Besides, there are several small scale units in the decentralized sector producing handicrafts, decoratives, twines, pulp and paper from jute and allied fibers and particle board from jute stick.

Export trend reveals that the USA, Belgium, Syria, the UK and Turkey have been the five major importing countries for Indian jute goods, which accounted for about 51 per cent of total value of jute goods exports. Other five major countries importing jute from India were Japan, Egypt, The Netherlands, Saudi Arabia, and Germany, which accounts for 18 per cent of total value of exports.

Exports of jute and jute manufactures from India, which ranks next only to Bangladesh, fetched the country Rs. 13,577.72 million in 2008-09 as against Rs. 13,116.30 million in 2005-06. Exports in 2004-05 were of the order of Rs. 12,410.54 million. Exports in 2004-05, represented a growth of 36.71 per cent over Rs. 9,077.80 million in 2002-03. Decorative jute bags, toys, wall-hangings and other ornamental products, made out of jute fabrics have a good demand in the global market.

From gunny bags and packing material to the glamorous world of high fashion, jute fabric has undergone a spectacular metamorphosis. Prabha Malhotra, a fashion designer, recently presented a new range of high fashion garments and accessories created from jute fabric blends. She has launched this rough and rugged sack material into the arena of high fashion. Until now, jute had been identified as a crude material used mainly for gunny bags. But over the last few years, jute has been blended with synthetics or other natural fibers to produce attractive decorative items, blankets, bags, table mats, wall hanging, etc.

Major items of jute production are jute yarn, jute Hessian, floor covering of jute and other jute manufactures. Jute yarn, which is spun out of jute fibers, is in great demand and in 2003-04, Rs. 2,306.04 million worth of jute yarn was exported to different countries. Burlap, or Hessian, which is a plain woven fabric, is used in a wide range of applications and is also exported all over the world, both in the form of cloth and in the form of bags. In 2003-04. Hessian, valued at Rs. 3,963.49 million was exported. Then comes sacking, which is used for bags of all types, with a portion being exported. Finally, there is canvas, the finest of jute products, used in India for protection from weather.

Nearly 60 per cent of India's exports of jute consist of jute yarn and Hessian. Only 40 per cent consists of floor coverings and other jute manufactures, such as bags, toys, wall hangings etc. Floor coverings worth Rs. 1,432.49 million and other jute manufactures worth Rs. 2,976.99 million were exported in 2003-04. Only 20 per cent of jute products are exported, while eighty per cent of the production of 1,610,000 tons per year is consumed within the country.

It is noteworthy that in seven years, exports of floor coverings have gone up sevenfold—from Rs. 476.48 million worth in 1999-2000 to Rs. 33,799 million in 2005-06. Exports of floor covering, however, declined to Rs. 2,516.34 million in 2008-09. Exports of jute Hessian showed a growth of 156 per cent to Rs. 4909.00 million from Rs. 1917.05 million, while that of other jute manufactures of 108 per cent to Rs. 2,525.49 million from Rs. 1,212.56 million in 1999-2000.

However, exports of jute yarn during the same period has gone up only by 25.11 per cent to Rs. 2,301.83 million from Rs. 1839.78 million. This means exports of value added products are showing much higher growth compared to basic product, i.e. jute yarn. In 2008-09, exports of jute yarn, Hessian, floor covering declined, the only item showing growth was 'other jute manufactures, which went up to Rs. 4,916.38 million from Rs. 2,525.4 million. Jute yarn and jute Hessian showed further decline in 2009-10, according to provisional figures available from DGCI&S.

Although in the years since the Second World War, jute has faced increasing competition from substitute packaging materials, jute industry in India has stood its ground. Before Independence, India had a monopoly in the production and export of jute. After Partition, however, three-fourths of the jute growing area fell in East Pakistan, now Bangladesh, while jute mills were concentrated mainly on river Hoogly, near Calcutta. Nevertheless, India embarked on a vigorous campaign to attain self-sufficiency in jute. The drive proved remarkably successful as by 1958 more than 90 per cent of raw jute consumed by Indian jute mills was produced within India. Besides West Bengal, other States, which have jute mills are Andhra Pradesh (7) Bihar (3), UP (3) and Assam, Orissa, Madhya Pradesh and Tripura (one each).

East Pakistan, now Bangladesh, emerged as a competitor in the manufacturing and export field. The importance attached to jute by Bangladesh can be seen from the fact that the country even has a Ministry of Jute. It is significant to note that while India was exporting only value added jute products, it imported raw jute worth nearly Rs. 712 million in 2008-9, which means that Indian mills were short of the raw material for producing jute yarn and jute products.

Coir and coir manufactures showed constant growth, going up to Rs. 7,594.84 million in 2009-10 from Rs. 1,999.65 million in 1999-2000.

Coir is used in making rubberized coir mattresses. Coir and coir manufactures worth Rs. 6,806.99 million were exported in 2008-09 as against Rs. 1,999.66 million in 1999-2000. Today needled coir fiber is used in making needled coir products, or manufactures, including clean mattress, using modern machinery and rubberized coir fiber, a blend of coconut fiber and natural rubber. These are much in demand as they are of environmentally friendly nature, of being recycled and bio-degradable. These products are currently being exported to the USA, Germany, the Netherlands, the UK, Italy, Spain, France, Canada Japan, Australia, South Korea, and West Asia.

The United States with imports worth Rs. 2,804.49 million from India in 2004-05 constituted a major market for India's jute yarn, hessian, floor covering of jute and other jute goods. Belgium, Turkey, The UK, Egypt, Germany, Saudi Arabia, The UAE, Australia and Japan were other major markets.

A look at figures of some other countries shows that export of jute yarn and jute goods have a good potential, given efforts at market development. To mention a few of them imports by Switzerland, Philippines, Russia and Singapore were rather miniscule to make a mention. In all these countries, Bangladesh appears to be out-competing India.

A vigorous marketing effort needs to be carried out to ensure that India's export of jute goods, particularly floor covering of jute, including jute carpet, and of other jute goods, are promoted. Exports of rubberized coir mattresses and other coir products also need to be promoted. Given that a large number of countries – over 140 — are importing our jute goods and that floor covering and other jute goods have shown good growth, it should not be difficult to double our exports from the present level of over Rs. 10,000 million in another few years.

11

Ores and Minerals, Non-minerals and Metals

(Ores and minerals - iron ore, mica and processed minerals—non-mineral–Plastic and linoleum products, Rubber and rubber manufactured products, glass and glass ware, paper and paper products, primary iron and steel, ferro alloys, non-ferrous metals, aluminium, chemicals and paints, enamels and varnishes, residual chemicals and allied products).

India is a major producer and exporter of iron ores, minerals, processed minerals, other minerals, metals and chemicals. Ores and minerals are largely raw materials, used in the manufacture of finished products. Besides ores, minerals and processed minerals, India's exports included primary iron and steel, ferro alloys, non-ferrous metals, aluminium other than products and chemicals and paints, enamels and varnishes and residual chemicals and allied products.

India's chemical industry is amongst the most competitive industries in the world. It accounts for 15 per cent of the total value added in the Indian manufacturing sector. The basic inorganic, organic and agro-chemical industry constitutes a major segment of the country's economy. Important chemicals in the category are soda ash, caustic soda, liquid chlorine, calcium carbide, acetic acid, methanol, formaldehyde, phenol and acetone. India is currently the largest manufacturer of pesticides in Asia, second only to Japan. Some 125 units are engaged in the manufacture of pesticides and over 500 are making pesticide formulations.

Dyes, intermediates, coal tar and chemicals, and inorganic, organic and agro chemicals form a large sector in India's *exports, nearly equal to drugs and pharmaceuticals, as also cosmetics and toiletries, which together with castor oil formed part of Chemicals and Pharmaceuticals Export Promotion Council (CHEMEXCIL). Drugs and pharmaceuticals have now formed a separate export promotion council (PHARMACIL).*

Inorganic, organic and agro chemicals is the largest item in value terms in CHEMEXCIL's portfolio, fetching the country Rs. 159,739.14 million in 2008-09 as against Rs. 72,481.92 million in 2004-05, doubling the exports of the items in four years. Dyes, Intermediates and coal tar chemicals came next with exports of Rs. 110,429.63 million in 2008-09.

India imported in 2008-09, organic and inorganic chemicals worth Rs. 561,254.44 million as against Rs. 309,211.38 million in 2005-06, artificial resins, plastic material worth Rs. 181,172.97 million (Rs. 100,399.41 million), medicinal and pharmaceutical products worth Rs. 86,747.99 million (Rs. 45,508 million), paper and wood manufactures worth Rs. 44,215.34 million (Rs. 22,468.82 million), printed books, newspaper, journals, etc. worth Rs. 20,162.79 million (Rs. 21,023.49 million), dying, tanning and colouring material worth Rs. 37,887,34 million (Rs. 22,258.99 million) chemical material and products worth Rs. 96,255.80 million (Rs. 46,597.27 million), fertilizer manufactured worth Rs. 547,905.39 million (Rs. 74,080 million), fertilizer crude worth Rs. 48,873.82 million (Rs. 14,068.68 million), sulphur and un-roasted iron pyrites worth Rs. 29,948.49 million (Rs. 6,020 million) and coke, coal and briquettes worth Rs. 459,479.86. million (Rs. 171,280.94 million).

Ores and Minerals

India exported during 2004-05 ores and minerals worth Rs. 203,892.3 million, which was a growth of 70.07 per cent over Rs. 119,883 million in the previous year. The increase over the decades has been hefty, considering that exports of ores and minerals (excl. coal) was merely Rs. 520 million in 1960-61. The real growth in fact came in 2003-04, when the exports of these items skyrocketed to Rs. 119,883.2 million from a mere Rs. 83,351 million in 2000-01, according to figures available from Chemicals and Allied Products Export Promotion Council (CAPEXIL).

Iron Ore

Among ores and minerals, the item which fetched real value was iron ore, whose exports were of the order of Rs. 147,255.58 million in 2008-09 compared to Rs. 118,148.4 million in 2004-05, Rs. 51,732.6 million in 2003-04 and a poor Rs. 17,210 million in 1995-96. Iron ore is India's largest item of export, both in terms of value and quantity, with China as the main market. Iron ore production in the country currently stands at 142 million tons, of which 78 million tons is exported every year, mainly to the neighbouring China, which imported 69.75 million tons in 2005-06 valued at Rs. 144,899.1 million.

Besides China, the other markets for India's iron ore included Japan with imports worth Rs. 16,343.42 million in 2005-06, followed by Republic of Korea Rs. 2,285.39 million, Romania Rs. 680.09 million, Pakistan Rs. 881.09 million and Netherlands Rs. 965.81 million. Another item notable in value terms in the country's exports was processed minerals, which fetched Rs. 36,194.09 million in 2004-05 as against Rs. 28,277.70 million in the previous year, according to DGCI&S.

In minerals and ores, the largest items of exports in value (Rs. 33,720 million) in 2004-05 comprised granite, natural stones and products. Again granite and products was the largest item in value (Rs. 25,450 million) in 2003-04, followed by slate stones (Rs. 1,850 million), marble and products (Rs. 1,620 million), and other stones and products (Rs. 4,800 million).

Ores

The third item included in bulk minerals are ores, including salt, coal and aluminium metal. Besides iron ore, chrome ore fetched the country Rs. 15,275.1 million in 2004-05, manganese ore Rs. 648.6 million, coal Rs. 2,308.6 million, bauxite Rs. 1,536.6 million, salt Rs. 1,350.0 million, aluminium metal Rs. 9,965.9 million, copper ore a negligible Rs. 0.1 million, zinc ore Rs. 2,500.0 million and others Rs. 1,090 million, according to figures released by CAPEXIL in its Statistical Profile 2004-05.

Non-minerals

In the category of non-minerals are plastic and linoleum products (dealt with under a separate heading in this chapter) and rubber manufactured products. Rubber manufactured products included cycle tyres and tubes, transmission and other belting, conveyor belting wee belts, hoses, hot water bottles, rubber gloves, rubber condoms, hygienic and pharmaceutical products rubber products, rubber coats and aprons for textile industry, rubber sheeting, auto rubber parts and heat resistant rubber elastic tapes.

Other items in non-minerals included paints, varnishes and allied products, glass and glassware, plywood and plywood products, ceramics and allied products, sanitary wares, pottery wares, roofing tiles, asbestos joinings, emery grain, cement clinkers and asbestos cement products, crushed bone fertilizers, graphite products, explosives, matches, dying and tanning extracts, coconut shell charcoal, activated carbon, super phosphate, other chemical fertilizer and urea.

Exports of paints, varnishes and allied products fetched the country Rs. 266,259.07 million in 2008-09 as against Rs. 18,879.80 million in 2005-06 and glass and glassware Rs. 44,823.35 million against Rs. 10,581 million in 2005-06. Others items for which information is available till 2005-06 from DGCI&S and CHEMEXIL, include plywood and plywood products, including wood and cork manufactures, Rs. 10,685 million, ceramics and allied products, including refectories, Rs. 7,176 million, sanitary wares Rs. 710 million, pottery wares Rs. 700 million, glazed ceramic tiles Rs. 1,300 million, roofing tiles Rs. 16 million, ceramic products Rs. 290 million, asbestos joinings Rs. 139 million, emery grain, powder and paste, Rs.180 million.

Among other items in non-mineral were cement, which fetched the country Rs. 6,175 million, clinkers Rs. 4,100 million and asbestos cement products Rs. 35 million, with aggregate exports valued at Rs. 10,310 million.

Bones

Exports of crushed bones, fertilizers, excluding super phosphate and urea, fetched the country Rs. 490.2 million. Besides crushed bones, with exports of the order of Rs. 183.4 million, items under the head included bone grist Rs. 29.5 million, horn meal and hoof meal Rs. 40 million, animal glue Rs. 39 million, meat and bone meal Rs. 26 million and other bone products Rs. 168.2 million.

Graphite

Exports of graphite products and explosives fetched the country Rs. 4,640.0 million in 2004-05, of which graphite products alone amounted to Rs. 4,200 million. Exports of explosives, which included detonator, detonating fuse and safety fuse, etc were worth Rs. 440 million.

Among non-minerals, the exports of other products fetched the country Rs. 1,289.0 million in 2004-05. The items under this head included matches (Rs. 520 million), dying and tanning extracts (Rs. 95 million), coconut shell charcoal (Rs. 65 million), activated carbon (Rs. 350 million), super phosphate, including other chemical fertilizer (Rs. 23 million) and urea (Rs. 20 million).

China is India's largest market for minerals and ores, having a 56 per cent share of its global market in 2004-05, while United States was the biggest market for non-minerals, having a share of 13.3 per cent. Japan (6.5%), UAE (5.3%), Italy (3.3%) and Republic of Korea (2.4%) were other markets for minerals and ores. For non-minerals the UAE (7.6%), the UK (5%), Sri Lanka (3.8%), Germany (3.3%) and Bangladesh (3.2%) were some of the other markets.

Region-wise, East Asia imported from India 75.2 per cent of minerals and ores in 2004-05 as against 69 per cent in the previous year and 25.8 per cent of non-minerals against 27 per cent in 2003-04. Next came Western Europe, importing 11.6 per cent of minerals and ores compared to 11.8 per cent and 20 per cent of non-minerals as against 20.7 per cent. West Asia came third importing from India 4.3 per cent of minerals and ores against 5.3 per cent and 17.7 per cent of non-minerals against 17 per cent.

The USA and Canada emerged fourth importing 5.7 per cent of minerals and ores in 2004-05 against 7.9 per cent in the previous year and 14.1 per cent of non-minerals against 13 per cent in the previous year. East Europe came next importing 1.9 per cent of minerals and ores against 3.5 per cent and 2.7 per cent of non-minerals against 2.9 per cent. Africa imported negligible proportion of minerals and ores (0.6%), while its imports of non-minerals was 11.3 per cent against 13.4 per cent in 2003-04. Latin America's imports of minerals and ores was minimal (0.1%), while its imports of non-minerals was 6 per cent.

Processed Minerals

Under the item "processed minerals", there were more than 18 items, the largest being calcined alumina, whose exports fetched the country Rs. 11,500 million in 2004-05 of a total of Rs. 17,349 million. Other items included barites Rs. 1,145 million, limonite (Rs. 800 million), feldspar (Rs. 640 million), aluminium hydrate (Rs. 580 million) and garnet (Rs. 500 million).

Processed minerals were imported by 156 countries. China again importing the maximum in 2004-05 (Rs. 11,065.2 million). Other major markets for processed minerals included the USA, Iran, the UAE, Netherlands and Russia.

Other Ores and Minerals

In other ores and minerals (items not listed), China again dominated with imports worth Rs. 16,119.73 million in 2004-

05 followed among others by Italy, Republic of Korea, Japan, Spain, the UK and the USA.

Agro-chemicals

China was again the largest importer of inorganic, organic and agro-chemicals with imports worth Rs. 15492.47 million in 2005-06, followed among others by the USA, the UK, Germany, the UAE, the Netherlands and Japan.

Plastic and Linoleum Products

Spurred by a whopping growth in raw materials, exports of plastics by India surged to Rs. 87,168.92 million in 2004-05 from Rs. 33,211.22 million in 2000-01, registering a growth of 162.46 per cent in four years. The growth in raw materials export during the period was 592.41 per cent to Rs. 51,827.7 million in 2004-05 from Rs. 7,485.11 million in 2001-02. This represents a decline in the proportion of export of finished goods over the years, which is not a very happy sign. The exports of plastic and linoleum products surged further to Rs. 124,821.31 million in 2005-06.

China has been a bulk importer of raw materials from India, with its imports of the item going up to Rs. 15,339.42 million in 2004-05 from Rs. 1,018.86 million in 2000-01. Its imports of raw material from India have been rising several fold each year from Rs. 36.49 million in 1998-99. India's decline in the exports of finished goods is a gain for China, which is its main competitor.

India's exports of plastic raw material in 2004-05 represented 68 per cent of its total exports of plastic products– Rs. 51,827.79 million out of a total of Rs. 87,168.92 million. Of the total export of raw material, China accounted for Rs. 15,339.42 million, or 29.59 per cent. China's other major import of plastic products from India included human hair (Rs. 2,059.81 million) and plastic moulded and extruded goods (Rs. 1,628.02 million). Plastic raw materials exported included PVC, polypropylene, polyethylene and polystyrene.

Besides human hair, India's export of plastic goods contained a number of interesting items, such as plastic bangles and imitation jewelry, toys, dolls and games spectacles frames and goggles. Among other items were plastic moulded and extruded goods, polyester film, plastic woven sacks, fabrics and bags, laminates, writing instruments, ropes and twines, moulded soft luggage items, PVC leather cloth and foam, PVC pipes and fittings, polylined jute goods, fishing nets, irrigation systems, floor coverings, plastic electrical accessories, plastic and cine X-ray positive and negative films.

Export of plastic bangles and jewelry went up to Rs. 7.53 million in 2004-05 from Rs. 3.38 million in 2000-01. The growth has, however, not been smooth. Exports of plastic bangles, gem and jewelry slumped to Rs. 91,000 in 2002-03 after growing to Rs. 6.97 million in the previous year. Although exports of the two items registered a growth to Rs. 2.55 million in 2003-04, it was still below the level of Rs. 3.38 million in 2000-01. India's exports of plastic human hair went up to Rs. 3,435.31 million in 2004-05 from Rs. 1,397.42 million in 2000-01. Exports of writing instruments went up to Rs. 2,194.65 million in 2004-05 from Rs. 1,700.82 million in 2000-01.

India's export of polyester film at Rs. 4,996.78 million in 2004-05 more than doubled from Rs. 2,312.05 million in the previous year. Export of plastic woven sacks, fabrics and bags went up by 72.95 per cent to Rs. 4,782 million from Rs. 2,765.25 million, while floor coverings went up by 47.42 per cent to Rs. 497.22 million from Rs. 337.28 million. There was a big jump of 135 per cent in the export of PVC leather cloth, which went up to Rs. 902.59 million from Rs. 383.81 million in the previous year. Growth in the export of PVC sheeting film was 350.46 per cent to Rs. 162.65 million in 2004-05 from Rs. 46.41 million in the previous year. Toys, dolls and games too recorded a hefty growth to Rs. 104.14 million from Rs. 53.65 million. Exports of only two items – hard recline lenses and polylined jute goods-registered declines.

Plastic goods and raw materials have been imported by over 150 countries over the years, most of them in insignificant quantities. CIS countries and Russia were the lowest importing region for India, buying merely one per cent of India's total exports of the items.

Imports of plastic goods by the United States, India's largest market in 2000-01, with imports worth US $223.61 million, showed a decline of 31.82 per cent to US $169.62 million in 2004-05. Its imports of plastic woven sacks and bags registered a growth of 618 per cent to Rs. 1,146.39 million compared to Rs. 159.45 million in 2000-01. Its imports of writing instruments too showed a growth of 302.53 per cent to Rs. 642.06 million from Rs. 159.5 million. At the same time, its imports of plastic raw materials went up to Rs. 1,459 million from Rs. 1,174.45 million in 2000-01. Its imports of plastic moulded and extruded goods, however, showed a decline of 426.76 per cent to Rs. 2,462 million from Rs. 7,690.7 million.

Imports by the UAE too registered a decline of a similar proportion (36 per cent). The UAE imported plastics worth Rs. 5,632.44 million in 2004-05 compared to Rs. 8,803.13 million in 2000-01. There was steep decline of 66.1 per cent in its imports from India of plastic moulded and extruded goods, which went down to Rs. 1,439.26 million from Rs. 4,246.02 million. There was, however, a whopping growth of 1,523 per cent in its imports of cine X-ray films to Rs. 39.67 million from Rs. 2.44 million in 2000-01.

Bulk of the imports by Turkey too comprised of plastic raw materials. Imports of raw materials by Turkey galloped to Rs. 3,295.55 million in 2004-05 from Rs. 56.57 million in 2000-01. At the same time, its imports of plastic moulded and extruded goods declined to Rs. 105.82 million from Rs. 131.72 million. Other items which registered declines in its imports of plastics were lenses, ropes, twines, yarn and bristles and writing instruments. Among items to receive good growth were floor coverings, laminates, polyester film, PVC leather cloth and toy, dolls and games.

Imports of plastics from India by Hong Kong more than trebled, going up to Rs. 2,715.85 million in 2004-05 from

Rs. 836.61 million in 2000-01. Again, there was a big jump in its imports of raw materials, which went up to Rs. 1,469 million in 2004-05 from Rs. 76.21 million in 2000-01. Its imports from India of plastic moulded and extruded goods too recorded good growth to Rs. 302.18 million from Rs. 33.27 million.

Another item, which recorded good growth was human hair, which went up to Rs. 588.68 million from Rs. 384.6 million. Other items to record good growth were polyester film, moulded soft luggage, ropes, twines, yarns and bristles and writing instruments.

Plastic moulded extruded goods, also known as otherme, which broadly contain 26 items, registered a growth of 9.5 per cent to Rs. 13,457.96 million in 2004-05 from Rs. 12,289.75 million in the previous year. However, the growth has to be viewed considering that in 2001-02, export of these goods was Rs. 15,297.2 million, according to figures available from the Plastics Export Promotion Council (PLEXCONCIL).

Otherme includes bags, bopp film, bottle caps, boxes, brushes, buttons, combs, crates and bins, engineering plastics, furniture, gifts, novelty and stationery, houseware, irrigation systems, mathematical instruments, multilayer film/sheets, PC sheets, packaging materials, PP mats, PVC Foam Board/ sheet, PVC rigid film, PVC rigid sheet, self adhesive tapes, surgical products, tarpaulins, thermo ware and zips.

The largest market for plastic moulded and extruded goods is the UAE, which imported goods worth Rs. 9,529 million in 2001-02. The USA happened to be the second largest market with imports worth Rs. 2,691 million. They were followed by Oman, Bangladesh, Germany, Kenya, Maldives, Kuwait, Cuba and Mauritius.

India needs to promote the production and exports of plastic goods and plastic moulded and extruded goods to realize the real value of export of plastics. Instead of exporting raw materials, which may earn foreign exchange in the short term, the country must look to long-term gain. India must learn from China, which has been importing not only plastic raw material from India, but also iron ore, turning it into steel, which is more valuable and fetches much larger returns.

Glass and Glassware

Exports of glass, glassware, ceramics, refectories and cement in 2005-06 amounted to Rs. 31,755.96 million. Items under the head included fibre glass, bottles and phials, glass beads and false pearls, ophthalmic lenses, float glass, vacuum flask and refills, glass lampware, scientific glassware and glass bangles.

Iraq turned out to be India's largest market for glass, glassware, ceramics and cement, importing Rs. 2,537.91 million worth of these items in 2005-06, followed by the USA, the UAE, Nepal, Sri Lanka, Qatar, Italy, China, Egypt, Yemen, France and Brazil.

Paper and Paper Products

Paper and paper products, the exports of which was of the order of Rs. 37,591.54 million in 2005-06, was another item under non-minerals. Items under this head included tissue paper, including cigarette paper, cellophane paper and paper board, including printing and writing paper, carbon paper, stencils, typewriter ribbon, computer ribbon and inkpad, exercise books and diaries, paper bags, paper boxes and containers of paper and paper board, playing cards, pencils, envelopes, writing blocks and letter pads.

Books, publications and printing, including printed materials, also formed part of non-mineral exports. Items under this head included books and pamphlets, newspapers and periodicals, job printing and printed material.

In paper and wood products, the USA was India's largest market in 2005-06 importing Rs. 5,925.83 million worth, followed among others by the UK, the UAE, Sri Lanka,

Nigeria, Italy, France, Bahrain, Germany, Malaysia, Spain, Korea, Egypt, Malaysia, Saudi Arabia, South Africa, Kenya, Singapore, Tanzania, Turkey, Kuwait and Norway.

Paints and Varnishes

Under paints and varnishes and allied products, CAPEXIL has listed 16 items, with the exports of printing ink fetching Rs. 3,200 million out of a total of Rs. 10,294 million in 2004-05. Titanium dioxide, synthetic resin, pigments and colouring material, zinc oxide, paints and varnishes, duplicating and fountain pen ink were among others. Exports of paints and varnishes fetched the country Rs. 18,879.80 million in 2005-06.

In paints, varnishes and enamels, the USA was India's largest market, importing Rs. 5,864.22 million worth in 2005-06 as against Rs. 4,048 million worth in the previous year, followed among others by Japan, Germany, the UAE, France, Italy, Belgium, the UK and the Netherlands.

India also imported in 2004-05 dying tanning, and colouring material worth Rs. 18,531.2 million and exported dye, intermediate and coal tar chemicals worth Rs. 53,461.24 million. The main sources of dying tanning and colouring material for India were China, Germany, Japan, the USA, Switzerland, Australia, Taiwan, Indonesia and Singapore.

India has had a hefty growth in exports of minerals, ores and non-minerals. However, in exports of items like iron ore, the needs of the domestic steel industry has to be kept in mind. With this end in view, the Steel Ministry wanted to limit exports of iron ore to 1.7 million tons as against the Commerce Ministry, which wanted exports of the order of 6.5 million tons. The R.K. Dang committee, appointed by the Steel Ministry, has in its recommendations said that domestic steel utilities be given priority along with those who intend to set up Greenfield projects of more than 10 million ton capacity.

It is perhaps taking into consideration the views in India over its imports of iron ore that Sino steel of China plans to invest Rs. 160,000 million in a five million ton green field steel plant in Jharkhand.

The growth in exports of ores and minerals has been steady, with exports worth Rs. 1,957 million in 1970-71, going up to Rs. 313,693.5 million in 2004-05 (estimated). There was a setback in this steady growth in 1998-99, when exports declined to Rs. 82,403.8 million from Rs. 87,637 million in 1997-98. The growth in 2004-05 was a hefty 44.97 per cent over the previous year. While keeping in mind the needs of the domestic industry, India should make all-out efforts to promote production and exports of minerals, ores and non-minerals and metals for which there is tremendous scope.

12

Items with Trade in Bulk

(Edible oil, Crude, LPG, naphtha, petrol, ATF, kerosene, diesel, fuel oil, bitumen and coal)

Vegetable oil fixed (edible) and petroleum, crude and products are two items with trade in bulk, only imports in the case of the former and both imports and exports in the case of the latter. While in the case of edible oil, efforts have been made to meet the huge demand for the commodity through production of oil from oilseeds, in the case of petroleum, crude and products, the effort has been to meet the cost of large-scale import of crude, through the export of petroleum products. Effort has also been made to produce bio-diesel obtained by mixing a portion of inedible vegetable oil with diesel.

Edible Oil

India is among the world's largest edible oil consumers and annually imports over four million tons making it highly susceptible to price fluctuations in the global market. Imports peak usually during the festive season, starting early August. The imports are mainly from Brazil, Argentina, Malaysia and Indonesia. India imported 6.72 million tons of vegetable oil fixed (edible) valued at Rs. 158,374.61 million in 2008-09 compared to 4.29 million tons valued at Rs. 89,609.86 million in 2005-06, according to figures available from the Director General of Commercial Intelligence and Statistics (DGCI&S) of the Ministry of Commerce.

India has been importing since the early eighties, 20 to 40 per cent of its edible oil requirements. To curb the heavy drain of foreign exchange resources, the government launched in 1986 the 'Oilseeds Technology Mission' (OTM) to increase the production of oilseeds. The main source of edible oil in India at that time were nine oilseed crops, of which groundnut, rapeseed-mustard and soybean were the main.

OTM aimed at increasing production of oilseeds through higher productivity. The government also maintained a stable market and price environment through market interventions and by managing imports. This provided the necessary encouragement to farmers to increase acreage under oilseed crops.

These measures taken together led to a rising edible oil output and stability in oilseeds and oil production. Edible oil production from primary sources went up to about 5.5 million tons in the oil year 1994-95 (November 94 to October 95) from 3 million tons in 1986-87; resulting imports coming down to negligible levels. Since oilseed crops were mainly grown in rain-fed areas, the focus on oilseeds benefited rain fed area farmers who had been otherwise shut out from the gains of the earlier 'Green Revolution'.

The programme came in for criticism among others from the World Bank. In a 1991 paper, the Bank argued that the government programme was economically costly, inefficient and unsustainable as production increases had been obtained in an environment where imports were controlled and domestic prices ruled higher than international prices. Its logic was that oilseed production in India did not have a 'comparative advantage. Hence, it was better to import oil and spend the country's resources in other areas.

After the programme had been in operation for several years, however, the Bank came up with a different assessment. In a 1997 report titled "The Indian oilseed complex: capturing market opportunities," the Bank considered the programme to be a 'conditional success' and agreed that the technology inputs provided in a protected oilseeds market had indeed resulted in increasing the productivity and improving the cost competitiveness of Indian oilseeds as well as stabilized the production. However, it still believed that the government's policy had left consumers in India bearing the cost, in terms of higher domestic prices of edible oil than international prices.

In 1994, in a change of policy, the government placed certain edible oil imports under the Open General License - which meant that imports could be made freely after paying duty. This was probably in anticipation of the commitments that India had made in GATT (General Agreement on Tariff and Trade predecessor to the World Trade Organization) relating to trade in agricultural commodities. Imports started increasing to satisfy some of the demand that could not be met earlier.

The World Trade Organization came into being in 1995 and adopted the agreements that had been reached by GATT members in the Uruguay Round. This included an agreement on agriculture that required reducing barriers to agricultural imports in the decade 1995-2004. As part of its obligations under WTO, the government removed quantitative restrictions on edible oil imports and replaced them with import duties. In succeeding years, even import duties were lowered rapidly, from 65 per cent in 1994 to 20 per cent in 1996 and 15 per cent in 1998.

The lowering of duties combined with a sharp fall in international edible oil prices in 1999 led to a flood of cheap oil being imported into the country, initially in far greater quantity than the requirement. By 1998-99, imports reached the level of 4.3 million tons, a ten-fold increase in four years.

One argument advanced in support of the policy of free imports was the benefit that consumers got through low prices and the increase in per-capita consumption of edible oils as a result of the lower prices. However, the flood of cheap imported oil had a deleterious effect on India's oilseed farmers. Oilseed prices crashed and remained depressed for the next three years. In 1999, newspapers reported massive distress sales of oilseeds by farmers at prices much below the

Minimum Support Price, with the government refraining from market intervention operations. The farmers responded by reducing the acreage under oilseeds. Domestic edible oil production from primary oilseeds fell sharply in the period 1996-97 to 2002-03.

The edible oil policy of the post-WTO period introduced a large element of instability into domestic production by completely exposing it to international price fluctuations. After seeing a continuous increase in acreage up from 18 million hectares in 1986 to 27 million hectares in 1994, the area under oilseeds production has remained around 26-27 million hectares, falling at times of depressed international prices. Productivity of land under oilseeds has also remained stagnant at levels of a decade ago. The OTM became dormant, never recovering from the body blow it suffered from the post-WTO policy regime.

In recent years, the international edible oil markets have come around full circle from the price lows of the year 2000. Indian farmers have not added acreage under oilseeds from the mid nineties because of the unstable market environment and withdrawal of government support. This has led to a large gap in supply and demand that cannot be bridged quickly. India is now dependent on imports for 40 per cent of its requirements at a time of sky-rocketing prices. As stated earlier, imports in 2008-09 were a high of 6.72 million tones, valued at Rs. 158,374 million as against 4.29 million tons at a cost of Rs. 89,609.87 million in 2005-06.

In this context, India needs to adopt a policy that would cater to the needs of the farmers as well as consumers. It should take steps to limit its dependence on imports and to encourage production. This would be nothing more than following the example of the United States and European countries, which have rid themselves of high dependence on imported crude petroleum by increasing use of bio-diesel, made from vegetable oils. If the US and European powers can limit their dependence on imports of crude petroleum for reasons of energy security, India can do the same for reasons of food security.

Castor Oil

While India has been importing edible oil, it has exported castor oil. The exports in 2008-09 were of the order of 357 million kg. valued at Rs. 21,287.18 million as against 254 million kg. valued at Rs. 9,397.38 million in 2005-06. The exports were mainly to the United States, China, France and Japan.

Petroleum

India, currently a net importer of petroleum, crude and products, is seeking to revamp its oil refining capacity to become a major exporter of petroleum products and to use export earnings to partly cover its import bill. An 'export-blueprint, drawn by the Petroleum Ministry envisages converting the present and planned coastal refineries into export-oriented refineries with large capacities so that export earnings pay for the import of crude oil.

India is a net importer of petroleum, crude and products. India's imports of these items during 2005-06 were valued at Rs. 1,996,730 million, while its exports were of the value of Rs. 499,740 million, according to official figures. The net imports, thus, worked out to Rs. 1,496,990 million. Of the total, imports of crude amounted to Rs. 1,717,020 million. Besides crude, India imported LPG, naphtha, petrol, ATF, kerosene, diesel, fuel oil, bitumen among others. India also exported these products.

India exported during 2005-06 petroleum products worth Rs. 515,328.01 million as against Rs. 305,181 million in 2004-05, which represented a good growth over Rs. 163,874 million during 2003-04.

Under the new strategy, presented in the "Export Blueprint" drawn by the Petroleum Ministry, coastal refineries, which are economic and competitive compared to neighbouring overseas refineries, would be equipped to focus on exports, while new inland refineries would be built soon to meet the hinterland demand-supply gap. Currently, the government incurs huge expenditure on account of moving petroleum products from coastal refineries to the hinterland.

The Ministry is exploring the possibilities of revamping Hindustan Petroleum Corporation's Vizag refinery capacity to 25 or 30 million tons per annum from the present 7.5 million tons and scaling up Indian Oil Corporation's proposed Paradip refinery to handle 50-60 million tons per annum. It wants to build large refineries by scaling up public sector refineries to be larger than the single private sector refinery. Reliance Industries' 33 million tons per annum refinery at Jamnagar in Gujarat is India's single largest refinery. The largest public sector refinery is IOC's Koyali refinery, with a capacity of 13.7 million tons per annum.

The Ministry wants inland refineries proposed at Bina in Madhya Pradesh and Bhatinda in Punjab to be quickly implemented to meet the hinterland demand, while the resulting surplus at the coastal refineries be exploited to the hilt by exporting their products.

India's installed capacity of 126 million tons exceeded the domestic demand of 108 million tons, resulting in exports that have grown from 8.4 million tons in 2000-01 to 24.23 million tons in 2005-26.

The coastal refineries have been exporting surplus petrol, diesel, naphtha, fuel oil to sustain their profits as well as earn foreign exchange.

Crude

Seventy per cent of petroleum refining industry's raw material–crude oil, is met through imports, which in turn accounts for 27 per cent of import bill. Oil refining industry is distinctive, where capacity addition would always be at the cost of a widening trade deficit. From a refining deficit country in mid-90s when India had to depend upon imported petroleum products to fuel the domestic markets, today it is in a surplus, leading to quantum jump in exports.

To cash in on the boom, Indian companies are pumping in big money into oil refining, aiming to increase the oil refining capacity by 61 per cent to 241 million tons per annum (MPTA) by 2012. With refining capacity growing faster than domestic demand, the country will only strengthen its present status as a net exporter of petro-chemical products. The consumption of petro-chemicals in 2012 is seen at 132 MTPA (excluding LPG, because it is imported).

The commissioning of Essar oils 10.5 million ton refinery at Vadinar recently marks another step towards India's emergence as a major hub of petroleum products. India's petroleum refining capacity will cross 150 million tons per annum this year, whereas domestic consumption is likely to be around 115 MTPA. Apart from expansions of existing refineries, major players are also putting up new projects that could take the capacity to more than 200 MTPA. Indian refineries are in surplus, when the world is facing a capacity crunch and high margins.

Indian Oil Corporation (IOC), India's largest refiner with 60 million tons is expected to reach 80 million tons by 2012. The expansion will come through a new 15 million ton refinery at Paradip and some expansions of existing refineries. On the other hand, BPCL has announced a 6 million ton refinery at a project cost of Rs.1,020,000 million. The project was to be completed by the end of 2009. MRPL is planning to expand capacity from 9.7 million tons to 15 million tons. MRPL is already exporting close to half its production.

LPG

India imported LPG of the total value of Rs. 70,420 million in 2005-06 as against Rs. 44,130 million in the previous year. India exported LPG worth Rs. 1,640 million as against

Rs. 3,060 million in 2004-05. Exports of LPG, however, began only in 2004-05, while the country has been importing it right from 1997-98.

Naphtha

India imported naphtha of the value of Rs. 5,400 million and exported the item of the value of Rs. 107,870 million in 2005-06. Export of the item was Rs. 11, 860 million in 1997-98, while its import was of the value of Rs. 11,360 million in that year.

Petrol

The country imported petrol of the value of Rs. 12,860 million in 2005-06 and exported it of the value of Rs. 58,430 million. Imports of petrol stood at Rs. 2,720 million in 1997-98, but galloped to the 2005-06 level with the expansion of the automobile industry in the country.

Kerosene

India imported kerosene worth Rs. 26,170 million in 2005-06 as against Rs. 43,910 million in 1997-98. Kerosene, which is of daily use all over the country, mostly in rural areas, is not being exported, which means domestic consumption is being met in a large measure through increased production at home.

Diesel

Diesel, which is increasingly being used in automobiles, was imported of the value of Rs.19,020 million in 2005-06 as against Rs.137,760 million in 1997-98, which again shows that production within the country was meeting a large part of the domestic demand.

Fuel Oil

India imported during 2005-06 fuel oil worth Rs. 29,990 million as against Rs. 2,520 million in 1997-98. It exported fuel oil worth Rs. 22,680 million as against Rs. 810 million in 1997-98. Thus, overall exports in 2005-06 were much larger.

Bitumen

India imported bitumen worth Rs. 220 million in 2005-06 and exported the commodity worth Rs. 250 million. It started importing bitumen only in 2001-02 when imports were of the order of Rs. 90 million.

Overall, petroleum exports are expected to exceed US $ 20 billion in current fiscal, as against US $9.5 billion in previous fiscal. With this development, the petroleum sector will emerge as the largest foreign exchange earner with a 16.2 per cent share in country's export basket. With the doubling of capacity at the Panipat refinery to 12 mtpa, India has added 16.5 million tons of refining capacity in 2007. As a result, the capacity of India's refineries has scaled up to 149 MPTA. Given the importance of exports, India needs to produce world class petroleum products.

Coal

India imported coal, coke and briquettes worth Rs. 143,709.47 million in 2004-05. The main sources of supply of the items were Australia, China, Indonesia, South Africa, the USA and New Zealand.

13

Trade in Services

Services account for over half of domestic production and provide about two-third of employment in the organized sector. Trade in services has grown more rapidly than merchandise trade since 1985. In 2004, while India's share in world merchandise export was 0.8 per cent, the corresponding share in world commercial services was 1.9 per cent. Services, accounting for 54.1 per cent of GDP in 2005-06, is a sector of crucial interest to India.

India, with its vast, natural resources, and huge base of skilled manpower combined with cutting edge technology, is fast emerging as a global leader. Today, Indian products and services are of international quality and globally competitive. India is today a reliable major sourcing base.

Services exports grew by 71 per cent in 2004-05 to US $ 46 billion. In 2005-06, with a growth of 42 per cent trade in services have been valued at US $61.4 billion. Growth has been particularly rapid in the miscellaneous services category, which comprises financial services, business services and commercial services.

In 2005, while India's share and ranking in world merchandise exports were one per cent and 29 respectively, its share and ranking in world commercial services was 2.3 per cent and 11 respectively. By growing faster than merchandise trade, services export constituted almost 60 per cent of merchandise trade in 2005-06. India's services export has been growing much faster than world services export. In 2000-2006, growth in India's services export was 38.22 per cent, while that of the world was 12.84 per cent.

With the spread of telecommunications and computer technologies, virtually all commercial services have become tradable across borders. The trend of globalization, reinforced by liberalization policies and the removal of regulatory obstacles, has fuelled steady growth of international investment and trade in services.

Given its strong position in Information Technology (IT) and ITES, and the competence of its professionals, India's efforts at negotiations at the World Trade Organization (WTO) have been to get binding commitments in cross-border supply of services (Mode 1) and movement of natural persons (Mode 4). In mode 4, India has been pushing for clear prescription of the duration of stay and the removal of the Economic Needs Test (ENT).

In the US $ 3.7 trillion world export of commercial services in the year 2008, the major exporters of services are the developed countries. Excepting India and China, which were among the top 10 exporters of commercial services in the world in 2008, the rest were developed countries. As in the case of merchandise trade, India has also improved its rank in commercial services trade. While India improved its rank in world merchandise exports from 28th position in 2006 to 26th position in 2007, in commercial services exports it has improved its rank from 10th position in 2006 to 9th position in 2007. China ranked 7th.

The share of India's services exports in the international market will triple in five years, with the volume surpassing the country's merchandise exports, according to Federation of Indian Chambers of Commerce and Industry (FICCI).

According to a study by FICCI, Indian services exports would be close to US $311 billion by 2012 and are expected to overtake the expected level of merchandise exports of $305 billion. The study adds that India's export of commercial services would cross that of China by 2009.

Currently, India exports services worth more than US $56 billion every year whereas its merchandise exports are over

$100 billion per annum. The services exports have been growing at an average rate of 28 per cent per annum of late while merchandise exports have maintained a growth rate of 22 per cent per annum during the same period.

The type of services expected to drive an accelerated growth over the next five years include software services, business and management consultancy services, architectural services, engineering and other technical services, tourism services and other professional services.

The FICCI study indicates that in terms of share in worldwide services exports, India would almost triple its share from the current 2.3 per cent to 6 per cent by 2012. Apart from this, the country's export of commercial services would cross that of China by 2009.

At present, China's commercial services exports of US $74 billion are more than that of India. The average annual growth rate of services in China over the past five years has been 19 per cent. Commercial services exports from China are, therefore, projected to be around $300 billion against $397 billion for India by 2013.

Describing travel, tourism and software as major services, Economic Survey 2004-05 says in 2003-04 travel accounted for 16.5 per cent of total services export. This, however, represented a steep decline from 36.9 per cent in 1995-96. Transportation too showed a decline to 13.1 per cent in 2003-04 from 27.4 per cent in 1995-96. Software, however, showed a good growth, going up to 48.9 per cent from 10.2 per cent in 1995-96.

Besides software in which India has already made an impact, there is good potential for export of many other professional service, like super-speciality hospital, satellite mapping, printing and publishing, accounting auditing and book-keeping services.

According to Economic Survey, there are 12 main categories and 156 sub-categories of services. The type of services that are expected to drive accelerated growth in the next five years include software services, business and management consultancy services, architectural services, engineering and other technical services, tourism services and other professional services.

Growth has been particularly rapid in miscellaneous services category, which comprises financial services, business services and commercial services, which include travel, transport and software.

A major category in software exports is manpower. Manpower export is a specialized profession that helps generate overseas employment for the already vast unemployed/under employed population in India. Manpower exporters mainly cater to the developing oil rich and wealthy the gulf countries, besides countries like the USA and the UK. They also cater to highly-skilled professionals including medical and para-medical staff. In the recent past, European countries like Romania, Poland, Slovakia, etc. have also opened up for manpower from India. The foreign exchange it generates from the overseas employment sector is unbeatable by any other export oriented industry.

Manpower is one of the services, which has an export promotion council (EPCOM). It is registered under Companies Act 1956 (under Section 25) as a non-profit-making Society representing Indian manpower exporters and allied professionals.

The constraints on potential opportunities in services trade include lack of set-up, like export promotion councils, other than for computer software and manpower, various visible and invisible barriers to services trade, visa restrictions, economic needs test, sector specific restrictions and selective preferential market access, through regional initiatives. These need careful examination in the context of requests and offers of different countries in WTO.

Further, two major areas where reforms can help in sustaining export growth are related to domestic regulations and reforms and market access for services. Domestic regulations perform the role of tariffs in regulating services trade. Disciplining many of the domestic regulations can help in the growth and export of services. The basic elements include licensing requirements and procedures, qualification requirements and procedures, technical standards and regulatory transparency. There are also visible and invisible barriers to services trade. Policy reforms aimed at removing these barriers to increase the country's market access to major trading partners along with policies, like marketing of services and successful services negotiations in WTO can help. As already stated in the ongoing negotiations at WTO under the General Agreement on Trade in Services (GATS), India has been trying to get binding commitments in cross-border supply of services and movement of natural persons.

14

Direction of Trade

(USA, Canada, China, UAE, EU, Iceland, ASEAN+2, Japan, BIMSTEC, Indo-GCC West Asia, Afghanistan, Pakistan, Africa, Russia, CIS & Mercosur).

The direction of India's trade with the outside world has undergone a sea change over the last several centuries. United States, which currently occupies the top position in India's trade was nowhere in the reckoning till the early years of the twentieth century. Nor was United Arab Emirates (UAE), which now holds the third position. China, India's northern neighbour alone continues as a major trade partner of India, holding the second position.

India has been carrying on trade with China, the neighbouring East Asian, the West Asian and east African regions since the earliest of times. China was perhaps India's earliest trading partner. As already mentioned in the chapter on "Trade-Ancient India," according to Zinru Liu, trade was almost entirely in luxury goods and was supported by the Chinese and Indian governments.

India also had trade relations with other ancient civilizations, like Egypt and Mesopotamia (today's Iraq). Trade with Europe followed and was of a much larger magnitude. The attack on India by Alexander the Great in 332 BC had far reaching impact on trade and commerce of the two peoples.

The Romans, first carried on trade with India through the overland route, via Anatolia and Persia. During the Sultanate period, articles of everyday use, as well as luxury articles were exported to Syria, Arabia and Persia from Bengal and Cambay. Arab traders shipped Indian goods to European countries through the Red Sea and the Mediterranean ports. Indian products were also sent to East Africa, Malaya, China and the Far East. Trade was conducted through overland routes with Afghanistan, Central Asia and Persia.

Trade with China and South-east Asia was mainly carried on through port of Sonargaon, now known as Dacca. Vijayanagar, which was the richest and most expensive state in the 15th and 16th centuries, enjoyed the most voluminous maritime trade with diverse countries, such as Persia, Arabia, Africa, Malayan Archipelago, Burma, China and the numerous islands in the Indian Ocean.

India also had trade relations with the Russian Empire during World War I. The Russian Empire has broken into Russia and Commonwealth of Independent States (CIS). Germany, Japan and USA entered the trade with India in the early 19th century, although there is a mention of pepper corns of the same vintage as was found in Berenike, being excavated in Germany during antiquity. There is also a mention of Australia being a market for jute goods in the second half of the 19th century.

India entered trade with different countries of the African continent and Latin America only in the early years of the 21st century. Firm details of foreign trade in volume, value and to regions is available only from the middle of 20th century (1960 onwards).

USA

India exported to USA goods worth Rs. 418,595 million in 2005-06. Its imports were, however, much higher in value terms at Rs. 768,281 million, carrying the two-way trade to Rs. 1,186,876 million, double the trade turnover of Rs. 562,840 million in 2000-2001. The two-way trade between India and the USA has shown a constant rise from 2001-02 when there was a marginal decline from Rs. 562,840 million in 2000-01.

United States' major imports from India included precious stones, diamonds and gold jewelry, woven apparel, knit apparel, miscellaneous textile articles (linen, etc.), fish and seafood (frozen shrimp), textile floor coverings (knotted and woven carpets), iron/steel products (household articles, cast iron, tubes/pipes), organic chemicals, machinery (taps, valves, transmission shafts, gears, pistons, etc.) and iron and steel (hot rolled, galvanized/coated steel, stainless steel, etc.)

Major items of imports by India from the USA included machinery (computers and components, gas turbines, telecom, etc), electrical machinery (recording/sound media), medical and surgical equipment/instruments, aircraft, spacecraft (small aircraft), precious stones, metals (diamonds, not mounted or set, jewelry), miscellaneous chemical products, organic chemicals, plastic, wood pulp, etc. (waste and scrap paper and paper board).

China

China has been India's trading partner from earliest of times. Currently (2005-06), China's two-way trade with India stood at Rs. 780,415.64 million, enabling it to occupy the second position in its trade with India. India's imports from China in 2005-06 was worth Rs. 481,166 million, while its exports to China was worth Rs. 299,245.12 million.

India's main imports from China were electronic goods, medicinal and pharmaceutical products, organic chemicals, non-ferrous metals, other textile yarn and fabrics and made-ups, machinery except electric and electronic, transport equipment, coal, coke and briquettes.

China's imports from India included plastic and linoleum products, primary and semi-finished iron and steel, inorganic, organic and agro-chemicals, machinery and instruments, cotton yarn, fabrics and made-ups and RMG of cotton and man-made yarn.

UAE

India imported from UAE goods worth Rs. 174,008.15 million in 2005-06, while it exported to UAE goods worth Rs. 380.388.46 million. India imported from UAE pearls, precious and semi-precious stones, gold, electronic goods, pulp and waste paper, metalifer ores and metal scrap. India exported to UAE tea, rice (basmati) and non-Basmati, spices, cashew, fresh fruits and vegetables, meat and preparations, marine products, drugs, pharmaceuticals and fine chemicals, cosmetics and toiletries, gem and jewelry, manufactures of metals, machinery and instruments, man-made yarn fabrics and made-ups, RMG of cotton and of man-made fibers.

EU

India's relations with the EU have developed exponentially in scope and intensity in recent years. The formal basis of the current EU-India relationship is the Co-operation Agreement in December 1993. In 2000, EU-India partnership took a quantum leap with the decision to hold regular summits. Since then, there has been a year-on-year increase in the number, frequency and intensity of contacts between the two sides.

European Union, which consisted of 15 member, countries has from May 1. 2004, been a union of 25 states, with ten countries from central and eastern Europe joining it. With a population of 455 million and a GDP of around Euro-9,712 billion, the enlarged EU will account for some 18 per cent of world trade.

Taken as a whole, EU is India's biggest trade partner. EU's exports to India in the year 2000 were Euro 14 billion, which were matched by a similar volume of exports by India, which included textiles and garments, precious stones, leather, food articles. EU's exports to India included jewelry, engineering goods, chemicals and metals.

United Kingdom and Germany continue to be India's biggest trade and investment partners within the EU. Besides the UK and Germany, India's trade with Belgium, Italy, France and Spain, particularly India's exports, was good. With the rest of them, particularly Luxembourg, Bulgaria, Estonia, Latvia, Lithuania, Slovakia, it was much below potential.

With the expansion of the EU to 25-member countries, the scope for trade and economic cooperation has expanded tremendously. The enlarged EU will have a single set of trade rules, a single tariff and a single set of administrative procedures, which will apply not just across the existing fifteen member states, but across the enlarged union of twenty-five. This will greatly simplify the dealings that third country operators have within Europe. Third countries would, thus, benefit from an increased single market and a simplified and enhanced access to the acceding countries' markets.

Export figures show that India's trade with acceding countries is on the increase. While the share of these ten countries in India's total exports is small, it is apparent that these countries are a growing market and need to be explored further. Some of the main exports from India to these countries are gems and jewelry, drugs and pharmaceuticals, leather and leather products, agricultural commodities, like tea, coffee, sesame seeds, tobacco, textiles and garments, plastics and linoleum products, machinery and instruments, manufacture of metals, metal scrap, organic and inorganic chemicals and electronic goods. The major imports by India are leather and ready-made garments, medicinal and pharmaceutical products, fertilizer, electronic goods, rubber, chemicals and industrial machinery.

ASEAN+2

India has focused on Australia and New Zealand as a market for its products for the first time with the launch of the programme "Focus ASEAN+2." The "Look East Policy," begun in 1991, had already brought the ASEAN countries in India's ambit. The 'Focus' programme is aimed at sensitizing various organizations like export promotion councils, chambers of commerce and industry, Exim Bank and ECGC in their trade promotion efforts for enhancing India's exports.

Over the years, India's trade with ASEAN has shown an increasing trend, both in exports and imports. India's exports to ASEAN have registered a high growth of 33.5 per cent during the year 2002-03 against India's global export growth of 18 per cent. However, while Singapore, Indonesia, Malaysia, Thailand and Vietnam have shown robust growth in imports from India, the same can't be said about some of the smaller countries, like Brunei and Laos. Further, while Australia has shown modest growth in its imports from India, New Zealand has in fact shown a decline.

There should be considerable scope of promoting exports to Australia and New Zealand considering that their imports of goods from India was worth Rs. 26,568.07 million and exports a meager Rs. 3,907.30 million in 2003-04. Their imports shot up to Rs. 36,358.62 million and exorts to 6282.38 million in 2005-06. The potential can well be imagined when one sees that the imports of a city state like Singapore from India was Rs. 240,196.52 million in 2005-006. The imports of Indonesia (Rs. 61,106.32 million), Malaysia (Rs. 52,439.8 million) and Thailand (Rs. 47,607.6 million) were also much higher.

India's exports to ASEAN, a ten-member grouping, comprising Malaysia, Singapore, Thailand, Myanmar, Vietnam, Laos, Cambodia, Brunei, Indonesia and Philippines, have risen from US $2.5 billion in 1997-98 to US $4.6 billion in 2002-03. India's exports to these countries have shown a robust average growth rate of 27.6 per cent during 1999-2000 to 2002-03.

A trend analysis of India's exports to these countries reveals that while Singapore continued to be India's leading export destination, India's exports to Malaysia, Thailand, Philippines and Vietnam, in particular, have witnessed good buoyancy in recent years. Between 1997-98 and 2002-03, India's exports to Malaysia have risen from US $491 million to US $747 million, to Thailand from US $345 million to US $711 million and to Philippines from US $239 million to US $472 *million. Vietnam has also emerged as an important export market, where India's exports have more than doubled from US $127 million in 1997-98 to US $337 million in 2002-03, according to figures available from the Directorate General of Commercial Intelligence and Statistics (DGCI&S).*

Based on India's export capability and import demand in ASEAN countries, commodities with export potential to the ASEAN countries include cereals and preparations, iron and steel, machinery–electrical and non-electrical—transport equipment, pearls, precious and semi-precious stones, organic chemicals, plastic and articles of plastic, marine products and manufactures of metal. The potential items for imports from the ASEAN countries include pulp and waste paper, coal, crude petroleum, natural gas, equipment for specialized industries, fresh and dried fruits and nuts, according to a Commerce Ministry publication.

Major commodities exported to Australia and New Zealand during 2005-06 included cotton yarn, fabrics and made-ups, gems and jewelry, ready-made garments of cotton, manufactures of metals, machinery and instruments, drugs, pharmaceuticals and fine chemicals and inorganic, organic and agro-chemicals. Australia, in addition, imported marine products. New Zealand also imported from India man-made yarn, fabrics and made-ups.

There is good scope for export to Australia of passenger motor vehicles, computers and computer parts, medicaments (including veterinary), telecommunications equipment, motor vehicle parts. Items of export interest to New Zealand include carpets, textiles, clothing and footwear, pharmaceuticals, iron and steel articles. India could also try to export to these two countries other items it is already exporting to ASEAN.

While India has already been having a growing trade with ASEAN countries, there is need to accelerate growth in trade with Australia and New Zealand. Both Australia and New Zealand have trade agreements with India under which joint trade committees have been set up. The two countries also have joint business councils (JBCs) with India, which are for regular interaction among business community on both sides. These together with efforts under the "Focus ASEAN+2" programme could help increase India's exports to the two countries, as also promote trade with ASEAN countries further.

India signed free trade agreement (FTA) with ASEAN in August, 2009. Under the agreement, India has agreed to cut import duties on tea and coffee to 45 per cent, pepper to 50 per cent, crude palm oil to 37.5 per cent and refined palm oil to 45 per cent. Rubber has been included in the negative list.

There is significant overlap in farm produce of these countries and Kerala – tea, coffee, rubber, pepper and cardamom.

The free trade agreement in goods is likely to further promote trade between India and the ASEAN. India has already presented to ASEAN a negative list of 489 items and "a highly sensitive" list of five items that has been accepted by ASEAN. Palm oil and black pepper figure in the sensitive list. Malaysia and Indonesia have pushed for lower duty on palm oil imports by India, which could be in the region of 40-50 per cent.

BIMSTEC

BIMSTEC, a grouping started by Bangladesh, India, Myanmar and Sri Lanka in 1997, now also includes Bhutan and Nepal. The name of the grouping was changed at a summit in Bangkok—initially named after the founding countries—as Bay of Bengal Initiative for Multi-Sectoral Technical and Economic Cooperation (BIMSTEC). At Pukhet, where a framework agreement on Free Trade Area (FTA) was concluded. Bhutan and Nepal were admitted as members of the grouping. With two members from ASEAN – Thailand and Myanmar—it is envisaged that BIMSTEC activities should be designed to form a bridge linking ASEAN with SAARC.

The summit decided to take steps for timely completion of Free Trade Area (FTA) negotiations in a bid to boost trade and investment in the region. Prime Minister, Dr. Manmohan Singh, who represented India at the BIMSTEC Summit in Bangkok had initially expressed misgivings about the FTA, signed by the Atal Behari Vajpayee government with Thailand, as it was feared that the Agreement would have an adverse impact on Indian industry, insofar as third country products may enter India through Thailand. Dr. Singh later clarified that he had been assured by his Thai counterpart, Mr. Thaksin Shinatwara, that this would not happen. The agreement specified that only those goods, which have their value enhanced by at least 40 per cent, would be eligible for lower import duty.

Thailand is the second country in the grouping with which India has signed a Free Trade Agreement, the first being Sri Lanka. In the case of the remaining countries, excepting Bangladesh, a framework agreement on FTA was signed at Pukhet in Thailand. The declaration at the Bangkok talks of timely completion of free trade negotiations.

The seven countries signed a joint declaration committing themselves to giving a fillip to trade and regional economic cooperation by a slew of measures, including development of infrastructure. They decided to facilitate travel within the region for business, exchange programmes and tourism through a business travel card, or visa and also sought to introduce a special BIMSTEC visa. As per the declaration, they would focus on specific areas of cooperation—including trade and investment, transport and communications and tourism. Exim Bank's latest Occasional Paper indicated high potential for increasing trade and investment between India and other countries of the grouping.

Regarding the FTA, the first phase of the agreement, involved 50 per cent cut in import duties on some 82 items. The duty was to be further halved in a year and reduced to zero from September 2006. The list of 82 items includes, apples, mangoes, durum wheat, air conditioners, household refrigerators, cordless telephones and electric fans. The reduction of duties on other goods would happen in phases thereafter and a comprehensive duty-free regime implemented.

The Exim Bank study, given in its Occasional Paper titled "BIMSTEC initiative: A study of India's Trade and Investment with Select Asian Countries," says since the formation of the grouping in 1997, India's trade with other countries of the group has witnessed a robust rise, with the total turnover (exports and import) rising from US $2.2 billion in 1997-98 to US $3.7 billion in 2002-03. India, says the paper, maintains "significant and continuous trade surplus" with the other BIMSTEC members, with the exception of Myanmar, where trade balance is in the latter's favour.

About infrastructure, Exim Bank is in the process of extending a line of credit for financing up-gradation of the Yangon-Mandalay Railway System and another to finance the development of information and communications technology in Myanmar.

The BIMSTEC countries, the Exim Bank study says, offer a market for a wide range of products which includes, among others, drugs and pharmaceuticals, machinery and instruments, transport equipment, gems and jewelry, manufacture of metals and iron and steel. For India, these countries can be important sources of inorganic chemicals, leather, natural rubber, vegetable oils and non-ferrous metals.

Indo-GCC

The Gulf Cooperation Council (GCC), comprising six states of Kuwait, Bahrain, Qatar, Saudi Arabia, United Arab Emirates (UAE) and Oman, is a major trading partner of India and has the potential of superseding United States, which occupies the top position in its trade with India.

Two-way trade between India and GCC in 2005-06 was valued at Rs. 881,290 million with India's imports valued at around Rs. 355,056 million and exports at Rs. 526,234 million. UAE was the largest trading partner, exporting to India goods valued at around Rs. 192,770 million and importing goods valued at around Rs. 380,388 million in 2005-06.

The industry body, ASSOCHAM, in a paper says that the dynamics of Indo-Gulf bilateral relations are changing. The Gulf is no longer just a destination for Indian job seekers. The UAE has emerged as a leading trade partner of India. Hundreds of Indian companies are operating from various free trade zones in the Gulf. But the trade has been limited to a few sectors. Many sectors are still left unexplored, which, if harnessed, can generate billions of dollars over the next 5 to 10 years.

The paper has estimated that Indo-Arab trade in goods and services is likely to grow to $150 billion by 2012 and could reach to $500 billion in the next 10 years. Import of petroleum crude from GCC countries will form a major part of India's import basket as manufacturing in the domestic industry will accelerate substantially, and lead to higher energy demand for the domestic industry, according to the chamber.

As in the case of ASEAN, India has been pursuing the signing of a Free Trade Agreement with GCC too. Both sides have expressed disappointment over the slow pace of talks on the issue. Hopes have, however, been expressed of an early conclusion of the talks, leading to signing of the agreement. "The India-GCC FTA should be given priority as already India is the second largest trading partner for GCC. The challenges are on both sides.. but it should happen as it would open up more opportunities," the Sultan of Oman is reported to have said.

West Asia

Trade between India and West Asian countries has grown by leaps and bounds, but it is yet to reach levels commensurate with the historic relationship that exists between the two.

For decades, India has been concentrating on promoting trade with the United States and Europe. The trend to look at regions like South East Asia, later at Latin America and Africa is recent. It is a happy augury that we are now focusing our attention also on West Asia, which has a huge potential for growth in trade and economy in general.

India has close historical, cultural and economic ties with the entire West Asian and Gulf regions. While West Asia is a lucrative market for India's goods and service, India is also a big buyer from the region. India buys oil, petroleum products, fertilizers, inorganic and organic chemicals, plastic materials, fruits and nuts, ores, iron and steel, silver, electronic goods, manufactures of metals, pulp and waste paper among scores of items.

Machinery and instruments, manufactures of metals, textiles including ready-made garments, rice basmati, gems and jewelry, plastic and linoleum products, glass, glassware and ceramics, rice basmati, meat and preparations are items India exports to West Asia.

India's total trade with the Arab region during 2007-08 was $87 billion, and this rose to $100 billion in 2008-09.

Africa

Relations between India and countries of the African continent have traditionally been close and cordial. Africa has always been a part of the Indian ethos for a very long time because of its close association with India's independence struggle, and also because a good number of its citizens are of Indian ancestry. However, commercial relations between the two have not grown commensurately. Distance, language barriers, incidence of civil strife and macro-economic instability have been among the reasons that affected the country's trade with the region.

Taking into account India's close relations with countries of the African continent, the Indian Government had announced on March 31,2002, a "Focus Africa" Programme with stress on seven countries of the Sub-Saharan Africa, viz. South Africa, Nigeria, Mauritius, Tanzania, Kenya, Ghana and Ethiopia.

A year later, the scope of the Programme was extended to all other countries of the Sub-Saharan Africa, where India had diplomatic missions, i.e. Angola, Botswana, Ivory Coast, Madagascar, Mozambique, Senegal, Seychelles, Uganda, Zambia, Namibia and Zimbabwe, along with six countries of North Africa, viz. Egypt, Libya, Tunisia, Sudan, Morocco and Algeria. As many of the missions in Sub-Saharan Africa are currently accredited to other countries in the region, the Programme in effect covers entire Africa, says a Ministry of Commerce and Industry publication.

India-Africa Summit, held in April 2008 bears testimony to the keenness of the two sides to further develop the relations. This was evident from the statement by Joseph Kabange, President of the Democratic Republic of Congo, who said that the summit should have been held four years back, i.e. in 2004. Prime Minister, Dr. Manmohan Singh, asked by Indian and African Journalists why the government held the summit only in 2008, said "Ever since 2004, when we came to office, we initiated the process and it took us time to come to this summit."

The summit ended with Delhi Declaration and Africa-India Framework for Cooperation. The main focus of the summit, as reflected in the two documents and the statements of leaders, was on economic cooperation and industrial collaboration. The Indian Prime Minister announced US $5 billion credit-line to Africa, which it was hoped would be for projects, announced at the summit. Further, leading Indian officials from industrial groups, like Ravi Kant from Tata group, Mr. Sanjay Kirloskar from Kirloskar group had meetings with Mr. Kabange and other leaders.

The Africa-India framework for cooperation approved at the summit pledged to boost trade and investment, share expertise in agriculture, science and technology, water management and education. The Indian Prime Minister announced duty-free preferential market access to imports from least developed African countries, including 34 such countries in mineral and oil-rich Africa. The products covered include cotton, cocoa, aluminium ores, copper ores, cashew nuts, cane sugar, ready-made garments, fish fillets and non-industrial diamonds.

It is yet too early to evaluate how the Focus Africa Programme has affected trade, particularly India's exports. Yet with five of the seven countries in the first phase, trade has vastly improved, i.e. with South Africa, Mauritius, Tanzania, Kenya and Ghana. Even with the remaining two countries, i.e. Nigeria and Ethiopia, it has shown improvement when compared to 2002-03.

South Africa occupies the top position in its trade with India. After near stagnation till 2003-04, India's exports to South Africa jumped to Rs. 67,600.03 million in 2005-06, recording 400.60 per cent growth over 2001-02. Growth in the imports of three other countries in the first phase has been quite good. It has been 243 per cent in the case of Kenya, going up to Rs. 25,525.4 million from Rs. 744.01 million in 2001-02., 172 per cent in the case of Ghana and 149 per cent in the case of Tanzania. In the case of Nigeria and Mauritius growth at 44.08 per cent and 13.06 per cent has been rather low.

Excepting five countries, brought into the programme in the second phase, i.e. in 2002-03, growth in India's exports has been quite good. The growth in 2005-6 over 2001-02 has been 435.63 per cent in the case of Libya, over 271 per cent in the case of Algeria and Angola, 231 per cent in the case of Botswana, 169.86 per cent in the case of Namibia, 166.59 per cent in the case of Madagascar, 156.28 per cent in the case of Sudan and 106.26 per cent in the case of Egypt. In the case of Morocco, there was a decline of 8.23 per cent.

In the case of countries, brought into the "Focus" programme in the second phase, the share has been rather poor, except in the case of countries like Uganda (6.69%), Sudan (4.57%) and Zambia (3.63%). It has been below one per cent in the case of countries like Libya and Mozambique (0.37% in the case of both), Morocco (0.73%), Tunisia (0.71%) and Algeria (0.57 per cent). In the case of rest, it has been below three per cent.

Excepting Morocco, Senegal and Sudan, India's exports to these countries in 2003-04 has shown good growth compared to 2002-03.

The government, various export promotion councils (EPCs) and chambers of commerce and industry have been doing their best in promoting exports to African countries. Under the 'Focus Africa' programme, the government has been extending assistance to exporters and EPCs to visit these countries, organize trade fairs and invite African trade delegations to visit India. Indian missions in Sub-Saharan African countries have been activated to focus on commercial issues as a priority. With these measures, it is hoped bilateral trade would receive a boost.

Russia

India's trade with the Russian Federation has increased from US $1,295 million in 2002-03 to US $3,309.78 million in 2006-07. However, apart from 2002-03, India has had a negative balance, which went up from US $245.88 million in 2003-04 to US $1,505 million in 2006-07.

An Indo-Russia joint study group has recommended increase in two-way trade to US $410 billion by 2010.

CIS

The Commonwealth of Independent States (CIS), formerly republics of the Soviet Union, offer vast scope for promoting trade with India. The "Focus CIS" programme, initiated by India's Ministry of Commerce seeks to tap the potential with the support of Indian Missions in these countries, their diplomats in India as also the Ministry of External Affairs.

Trade between India and nine CIS countries has grown by only 45 per cent to Rs. 21,879 million in 2002-03 as compared to Rs. 15,005 million in 1995-96, according to figures available from Directorate General Commercial Intelligence and Statistics (DGCI&S). The maximum value of trade has been with Ukraine—Rs. 13,290 million in 1995-96 and Rs. 13,960 million in 2002-03 – showing minimal growth. On the other hand, trade with Kyrgyzstan (Rs. 2.18 million), Armenia (Rs. 10.74 million) and Azerbaijan (Rs. 10.63 million), although miniscule, has surged to Rs. 731 million, Rs. 128 million and Rs. 501 million respectively in 2002-03. Trade with Kazakhstan , Turkmenistan and Uzbekistan has been modest, but still needs to be improved a great deal.

It is worth noting that India's aggregate exports to these nine countries of Rs. 8,405 million is less than to countries like Indonesia (Rs. 39,970.29 million), Iran (Rs. 31,714.74 million), Malaysia (Rs. 36,140.48 million), Nepal (Rs. 14,384.12 million), Nigeria (Rs. 21,770.15 million), Philippines (Rs. 22,842.92 million), Sri Lanka (Rs. 44,566.35 Million), Sudan (Rs. 5,078.2 million), Turkey (Rs. 17,804.29 million), Vietnam (Rs. 16,316.29 million) and Yemen (Rs. 7,934.39 million) to name just a few countries, which could invite comparison with the CIS countries.

In pursuance of the programme "Focus CIS", Federation of Indian Export Organizations (FIEO) organized a Round Table in September 2003 in which ambassadors of Belarus, Ukraine, Kyrgyzstan, Turkmenistan, Uzbekistan and Kazakhstan participated. As per the announcement at the round table, a business delegation to four CIS countries was undertaken. The four countries were Azerbaijan, Kazakhstan, Kyrgyzstan and Uzbekistan. During the tour, buyer-seller meets in these countries were organized and MOUs signed. Wide-ranging discussions were also held with leading businessmen, policy-makers and senior officials.

The 16-member business delegation to these countries, led by FIEO Director General, Mr. G. Balachandran, generated *enquiries worth Rs. 1,434 million (US $31.19 million) in areas like veterinary medicines, perfumes, cosmetics, pharma/lab equipment/hospital equipment, flavors, healthcare products, agro chemical, leather products, mining, information technology (IT) and other software related services, out of which Rs. 129.5 million (US $2.77 million) is being finalized. The enquiries are substantial, considering that the total value of exports to these countries from India at present is Rs. 3,496 million (US $75.26 million) and shows that the exports could be increased substantially.*

India's imports from these countries consists mostly of agricultural produce, minerals, metalifer ores and metal scrap, manufactures of metals, organic chemicals, paper board and manufactures, while its exports included tea, leather garments and goods, plastic and linoleum products, transport equipment, machinery and goods, readymade garments of silk, cotton, manmade yarn, electronic goods, drugs and pharmaceuticals, cosmetics and toiletries, footwear of leather and tobacco manufactured and un-manufactured.

Kazakhstan

During the buyer-seller meet at Almaty, delegates reported receiving good business enquiries for their products like fuel injection equipment and spare parts, perfumes and cosmetics, veterinary medicines like de-wormers and antibiotics, flavours and industrial gaskets. Public sector companies like Bharat Earth Movers Ltd. were sounded about opening a representative office in Kazakhstan for bulldozers and excavaters. CMC Limited, which is the premier information technology company and part of the Tata Group, received enquiries for development of software/IT solutions in fields like computer networking, insurance, container and freight management, computer software solution, etc. Trade between the two countries, which had been stagnating at US $60 million, is expected to increase to US $70 million this year, according to Mr. Vidya Sagar Verma, Indian ambassador to Kazakhstan.

At the buyer-seller meet organised for the Kazakhstan business delegation to India, it was noted that the present bilateral trade, of US $60 million, was too small. The two sides had identified the areas of IT, oil and natural gas and pharmaceuticals for cooperation. Indian pharmaceutical companies, it was noted, had successfully established their base in Kazakhstan as a result of this initiative.

Kyrgyzstan

In Bishkek, capital of Kyrgyzstan, the Deputy Prime Minister, Mr. Bazarbai Mambetov, invited Indian businessmen to invest in Kyrgyzstan in fields like pharmaceuticals, energy, food processing, mineral exploration and take benefits of various liberalised measures like low tax structure, low customs duty and proximity to other CIS countries. The Deputy Minister for Foreign Trade of Kyrgyzstan, Ms Zhanil Tumenbaeva, suggested that Kyrgyzstan could be looked at by Indian businessmen as a hub for promoting trade with third world countries.

At buyer-seller meets interest was shown in India's electronics engineering, IT, textiles, pharmaceuticals, drugs and a host of other items. Proposals for investment of around US$ 50 million in sectors such as mining and food processing were also made at the meet.

Azerbaijan

At a buyer-seller meet, organised at Baku, capital of Azerbaijan, Indian businessmen were told that with Azerbaijan on the path of privatisation, the time was opportune for Indian companies to set up manufacturing bases and establish business contacts, particularly in areas like oil and natural gas, insurance, banking, information technology, infrastructure development (especially in the fields of construction, hospitals and roads) and tourism infrastructure. Mr. Alihusaein. Shaliyev, Deputy Director in the Ministry of Economic Development, stressed that Azerbaijan's proximity to

European countries and CIS could make it a hub for promoting India's trade.

At buyer-seller meet , businessmen of Azerbaijan, showed interest in establishing contacts in the areas of pharmaceuticals, agro-chemicals, veterinary software/hardware development, computer education, telecommunications, food processing, electronics, textiles and a host of other items.

Uzbekistan

At an MoU signing ceremony at Tashkent, Indian businessmen were asked to consider taking up processing of cotton in Uzbekistan as only 20 per cent of its overall production was processed. Indian entrepreneurs could utilize Government of India's credit-line, loans from World Bank and other funding agencies, Indian Ambassador, Mr. Sharat Sabharwal was reported as saying. The Director General FIEO, Mr. Balachandran, suggested reduction in the registration charges for pharmaceutical products. So far, 35 joint ventures had been established between the two countries, he said, adding that with the visits of Indian business delegation, more business could be expected to flow in particularly in the areas of information technology, infrastructure, mining and pharmaceuticals.

To expand India's presence in CIS market, FIEO has suggested opening of a land route to these countries via Pakistan and Afghanistan, i.e. via Srinagar, Muzaffarabad, Peshawar and Kabul. The Afghan Government could further extend the road up to Termez to the Uzbekistan border. For this both the Pakistan and Afgthanistan need to be approached. At present, the cost of sending a container to CIS countries and parts of East Europe is almost US $4,500 (20ft container) and US $6,800 (40ft., container).

Mercosur

India's recent trade agreement with the Latin American grouping, Mercosur, is in line with the country's trade policy of "Focus Latin American Countries" and would ultimately lead to free trade between the grouping and India. The agreement was followed by a Preferential Trade agreement (PTA) and would lead to a Free Trade Agreement, which is expected to boost trade with it, particularly India's exports.

The grouping, which covers practically the whole of South America, was formed in 1991 with Argentina, Brazil, Paraguay and Uruguay integrating their economies. Later, five other Latin American countires – Chile, Bolivia, Colombia, Peru and Venezuela—have fallen into different stages of association with Mercosur. With these countries, the grouping covers practically the whole of South America, leaving behind only the six smaller countries—Guyana, Surinam, French Guyana, Paraguay, Trinidad Tobago and Equador outside the grouping.

In strength just behind North American Free Trade Agreement (NAFTA) and the European Union (EU), member states of Mercosur signed the protocol of Montevideo in 1997 advocating that within ten years, all restrictions on trade and services will be phased out. A common passport has also been proposed to facilitate travel across member countries.

India's exports to the nine countries has grown from Rs. 7,949 million in 1995-97 to Rs. 37,855.39 million in 2002-03. As against this India's total exports to five other Latin American countries in 2002-03 was just Rs. 2,487 million.

Brazil, the largest among the countries in South America, is the economic backbone of Mercosur. It is the biggest market for India in Mercosur, accounting for Rs. 23,182.29 million of its total exports of 37.855.39 million to the grouping. Chile, lying along more than half of the western coast of South America is the second largest trade partner with imports worth Rs. 3,479.22 million from India.

Argentina, though much larger in size and lying diagnally along with Chile, imported from India goods worth Rs. 8,832.77 million in 2005-06. Bolivia is the smallest trade partner, importing from India goods worth Rs. 290.20 million. Venezuela, almost of the same size imports goods worth Rs. 81.32 million.

In the post WTO world, where preferential trade agreements are flourishing, this agreement has even more potential. It can help identify alternate and sometimes cheaper sources of goods between the trading partners. This agreement can, thus, also be used as a tool for strategic reasons. It also helps to facilitate cooperation between the weaker developing countries and help the South build a joint economic perspective.

Four countries of Mercosur, Argentina, Brazil, Uruguay and Paraguay, hold a population of almost 200 million (Brazil 150, Argentina 33, Paraguay 4.5 and Uruguay 3.1), a total area of 11,863 sq. kms, a GNP of over US $700 billion and foreign trade of US $120 billion. Intra-regional trade within Mercosur is being gradually liberalized.

Tariff on 90 per cent of intra-regional trade has been removed, with Common External Tariff (CET) ranging from 0.20 per cent. Since the signing of the Asuncion Treaty for forming Mercosur in 1991 inter-regional trade has almost tripled from US $ 5.1 billion to US $ 14.38 billion in 1995, while trade with the rest of the world has increased from US $67 billion to US $120 billion.

There is tremendous scope for the export from India of transport equipment, including components. Trade in automobiles and auto parts accounts for 30 per cent of total intra-regional trade. Other items with good export potential are drugs and pharmaceuticals, ready-made garments (RMG) of cotton and other fibres, inorganic, organic and fine chemicals, rubber manufactured products and leather footwear. The advantage to India from PTA and FTA with Mercosur would be that exports to one country could reach the length and breadth of South America, with countries other than the four original members set to join the grouping.

The conclusion of PTA and FTA would lead to tariff concessions on a reciprocal basis and mutual reductions in customs duties should follow soon after. For India, this offers major trading possibilities since Mercosur is the third largest common market in the world, after NAFTA and the EU. India should exploit its relations with Mercosur to the maximum to promote its exports to the distant South American countries in tune with "Focus LAC" programme of its trade policy.

A review of trade relations between India and other countries and regions shows that there are tremendous opportunities for the expansion of trade. There is scope for growth not only in the case of counties of the African continent, but also with Russia and the CIS countries, which have had thriving trade before the disintegration of the Soviet Union. Trade opportunities with Mercosur remain largely unexplored.

Although India has had trade relations with China and the neighbouring ASEAN for ages, scope for expansion nevertheless exists. The government and the business community are no doubt alive to the situation and are making efforts in the direction of achieving a reasonable share of world trade. Nonetheless, there is need for intensifying these efforts.

15
Revival of Barter

Barter, the oldest form of trade, where goods are exchanged for goods, without bringing in money, is being revived. The system allows cash-free buying and selling. The current global recession has fuelled barter trade and the trend is gaining momentum in India as well. India has been carrying on barter trade among others with China and Myanmar for ages.

In today's internet economy, barter is being promoted by the portal, B2B which is giving a new life to barter. Internet service provider, Net4India, has a 70 per cent stake in the portal and will invest US $3.5 million in the venture over a period of three years. "In the current global downturn, the global barter exchange companies are growing at 15 to 60 per cent and the same trend is fast catching up in India too,' the CEO of Bartermaniac. Co, Mr. Vipul Rawal, is reported to have said.

Net4Barter allows companies to trade excess stocks and capacities with goods and services. While barter did exist as a form of business transaction in unorganized forms, organized barter networks can help open up new avenues for businesses.

Despite the Sino-Indian border tension, the annual India-China barter trade at Taklakot mart in Tibet continued smoothly, with both sides reportedly exchanging goods worth Rs. 20 lakh in 2009. The Indo-Tibet barter trade, which was resumed in 1992 after a gap of 30 years following the 1962 war, reached Rs. 140 million mark in 2004. But after the ban of certain items like livestock and Chinese silk, trade is gradually declining. Traders had been seeking lifting of the ban on import of items like Chinese raw silk and livestock, which are in good demand in India. The import of livestock has been banned since no quarantine facility is available at Gunji, the Indian mart at Pithoragarh.

So far as trade between India and Myanmar is concerned, barter has been given a boost with India and Myanmar sealing a deal to expand the current list of items for barter trade under the India-Myanmar Border Trade Agreement to 40, besides converting border trade at Moreh-Tamu and Zokhawthar-Rhi border points to normal trade, paving the way for trade at Most Favoured Nation (MFN) rates for all goods barring a handful of restricted items. The Joint Trade Committee further decided to open border trade at a new border point Avakhung (Nagaland) - Leshi (Myanmar).

Coming back to internet helping promote barter, bartermaniac.com has launched a barter exchange named India Barter Exchange (IBX). The exchange offers membership to business, including professionals offering various services. Professionals, like lawyers, doctors, chartered accountants, or those who offer services like recruitment, housekeeping, transportation, security, IT hardware and maintenance, restaurants as also manufacturers and traders can join the exchange by paying a nominal annual fee. The moment anyone becomes a member of the 'Barter Club,' he is eligible to a credit of say Rs. 15,000 barter, Mr. Rawal is reported to have said.

While businesses are becoming more receptive to the idea of barter, it is still a fraction of India's annual commerce (10 to 12 per cent). Nearly 30 per cent of the world business is barter and 65 per cent of Fortune 500 companies engage in barter in one form or another, Rawal is reported to have said.

While one-to-one bartering is practised between individuals and businesses on an informal basis, organized barter exchanges have developed to conduct third party bartering. The barter exchange operates as a broker and a bank and each participating member has an account, which is debited when purchases are made and credited when sales are made.

Barter has, thus, developed into a sophisticated tool to help businesses increase their efficiencies by monetizing their unused capacities and excess inventories. The worldwide organized barter exchange has grown to a US $8 billion a year industry and is used by thousands of businesses and individuals. The advent of internet and sophisticated relational database software programs has further advanced the barter industry's growth.

Organized barter has grown throughout the world to a point now, where virtually every country has a formalized barter and trade network of some kind. Complex business models based on the concept of barter are today possible since the advent of Web 2.0 technologies.

A trade or barter exchange is a commercial organization that provides a trading platform and book-keeping system to its members or clients. The member-companies buy and sell products and services to each other using internal currency known as barter or trade dollars. Businesses in barter earn trade credits, instead of cash, that are deposited into their account. The exchange plays an important role as they provide record-keeping, brokering expertise and monthly statements to each member. Over 350,000 businesses in the United States are estimated to be involved in barter exchange activities. There are approximately 400 commercial and corporate barter companies serving all parts of the world. There are two industry groups, the National Association of Trade Exchanges (NATE) and International Reciprocal Trade Association (IRTA), both offering training and promoting high ethical standards among their members. Each has its own currency, Banc in the case of NATE and IRTA's UC or Universal Currency.

Net4Barter has set up six offices across the country. The venture will operate both online, through its site www.net4 barter.com, or offline through trade representatives. Offline, companies can register their products and services and their terms and conditions with its offices, which will then be evaluated to facilitate the barter transaction.

Net4Barter has already roped in clients like Bausch & Lomb, Kellogy's, Hyatt, India Today and UTV, for whom it has done a transaction of Rs. 2.5 million. India is, thus, moving ahead fast to make use of barter for promoting trade. With the use of internet, barter need not remain confined to transactions between two individuals. Considering the usefulness of the system, it should be used as much as possible for promoting trade.

Index

F

W

Y

Z